Leuven's College Laboratories

KU LEUVEN
FACULTY OF SCIENCE

Minderbroedersstraat 4, B-3000 Leuven (Belgium)

ISBN 978 94 6270 433 6 (paperback)
eISBN 978 94 6166 549 2 (ePDF)
eISBN 978 94 6166 578 2 (ePub)

https://doi.org/10.11116/9789461665492
D/2024/1869/52
NUR: 695, 693

Book design: Stéphane de Schrevel
Cover illustration: Jobard, J. B. A. M., and J. Collon. Plan Der Stad Leuven. [Bruxelles: Jobard, 1825]
Map pp. 4-5: Felix Vanderleenen
Translation: John R.J. Eyck

GEERT VANPAEMEL

LEUVEN'S COLLEGE LABORATORIES

AN URBAN WALKING GUIDE THROUGH 600 YEARS OF SCIENCE

LEUVEN UNIVERSITY PRESS

usselsestraat
Minderbroedersstraat

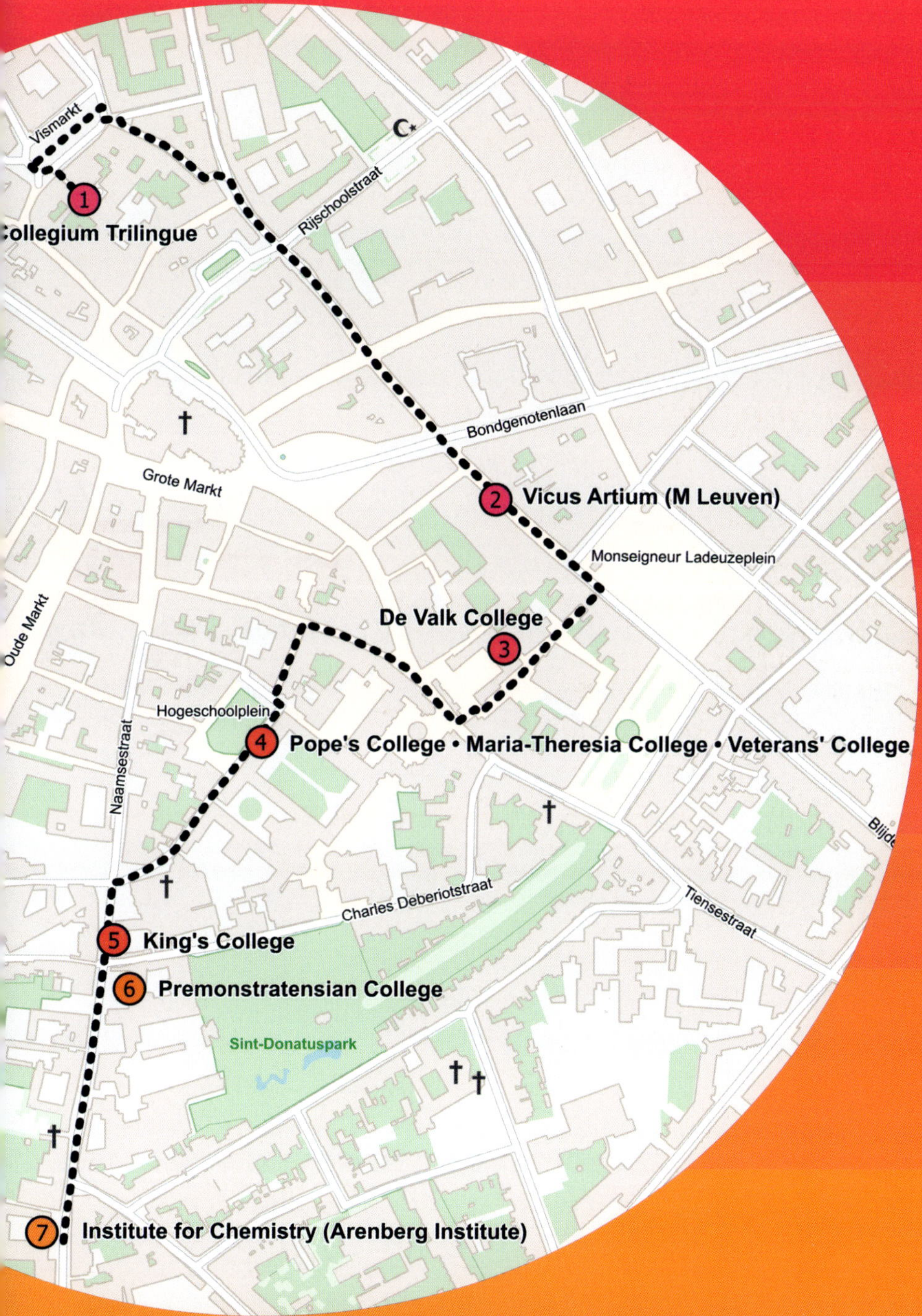

Vismarkt
Rijschoolstraat
1 Collegium Trilingue
Bondgenotenlaan
Grote Markt
2 Vicus Artium (M Leuven)
Monseigneur Ladeuzeplein
De Valk College
3
Oude Markt
Hogeschoolplein
4 Pope's College • Maria-Theresia College • Veterans' College
Naamsestraat
Charles Deberiotstraat
Tiensestraat
5 King's College
6 Premonstratensian College
Sint-Donatuspark
7 Institute for Chemistry (Arenberg Institute)

FOREWORD

On the eve of World War I, the Faculty of Sciences (which included the Special Schools for engineers as well as the Agriculture School) had around thirty laboratories. Most of them were housed in colleges that dated from the eighteenth century. As unsuitable as these locations were for installing modern labs, some of them remained in use until long after World War II. Even today, the laboratories for Animal Physiology and Neurobiology, as well as those for Ecology, Evolution, and Biodiversity Conservation, are located in the old King's College and the more recent Coal Museum nearby.

The history of laboratories at Leuven reveals a university that is continually evolving and responding to developments in the sciences. Surveying six centuries of scientific research makes clear how laboratories – literally – claimed their place at the university, and how they challenged the university administrators in terms of matériel and finances. It is a story of building and rebuilding, inventiveness and creativity, enterprising professors and their unrelenting complaints about lack of space and antiquated facilities.

In this walking guide, we'll be taking a tour of this history through seven moments in time, namely, seven colleges that were once flourishing workplaces for science: the Collegium Trilingue, the Vicus Artium, the De Valk College, the Pope's College and Maria-Theresia College, the King's College, the Premonstratensian College, and the Arenberg Institute. At the same time, we'll trace the historical development of scientific research at Leuven university, stopping to notice features typical for these laboratory colleges.

The itinerary proposed is about two kilometers long. The first three stops have to do with the Old University (1425–1797), stops 4 to 6 with the State University (1817–1835) and the Catholic University (1834–1968). The very last stop illustrates the exodus of the laboratories to the suburban campus in Heverlee.

At every stop, you'll get information about the architectural history of the college. Correspondingly, we'll shed light on the context for the scientific research in each college. The texts can be read separately, meaning sometimes it was necessary to repeat ourselves. Here and there, the text also goes into detail on the laboratories for medicine, the Special Schools for engineers and the Agriculture School. These last two institutions were part of the Faculty of Sciences until the mid-twentieth century. References to the medical labs are made only in connection with scientific research laboratories (anatomy, physiology, embryology, pharmacology, etc.), where scientists were often also involved. Clinical or strictly pathological laboratories are not taken into account.

By mid-2026, the last laboratory for the Faculty of Sciences will vanish from Leuven's town center. Commemorating six centuries of science at the heart of the town and the university, this walking guide fits within the framework of initiatives the Faculty is undertaking for the university's 600th anniversary celebrations. It will make those times both tangible and accessible by enriching the visible architectural remains of the past with the intangible stories of those who lived in those buildings. In the back of the book, we've included a short reading list for everyone inspired to learn more.

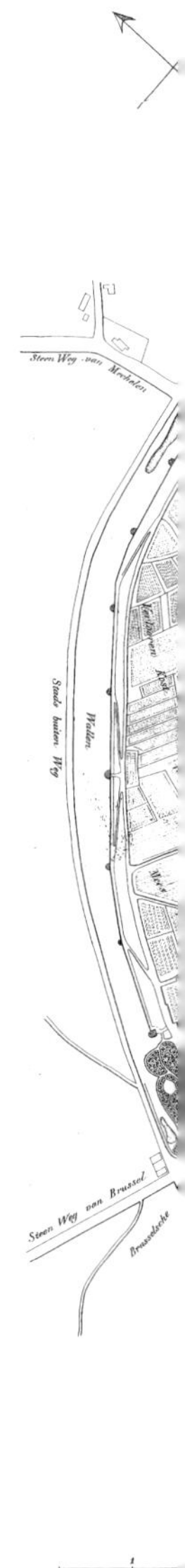

Stads buiten Weg
Stads Buiten Weg
Diestersche Poort
Sᵗᵉ Marcus Klooster
Castelynen Veld
Vleminckx Veld
Karthuizers Klooster
Wallen
Dyle R.
5,000 Ellen.

STOP NO. 1

COLLEGIUM TRILINGUE

→ Busleidengang 6

THE CRADLE OF HUMANISM AND SCIENCE

"At [Leuven]," Erasmus wrote in 1521,"the climate is agreeable, and there could not be a more peaceful place for study anywhere. Nowhere do the young show more enthusiasm for good literature, and many of them make wonderful progress, while the devotees of ancient ignorance protest in vain."[1] In view of his acute conflicts with Leuven's theologians, we might doubt Erasmus's sincerity when he wrote down these words of praise. Even so, Erasmus had a good reason for bearing a fondness for Leuven. Four years before, he had succeeded in establishing a new college in Leuven, one that was wholly dedicated to the study of the three 'holy' languages: Latin, Greek, and Hebrew. And this Collegium Trilingue (Three-Languages College) was much more than a regular instructional college. It became the birthplace of the humanistic movement that would thoroughly redraw the lines of scientific thinking, both at the university and far beyond.

Erasmus had first set foot in Leuven in 1498. He had the intention of settling in Leuven, though nothing came of it at that time. He arrived in the university town for a second time in 1502, and was warmly received. He was even offered a professorship, but he declined. The professorial life was nothing for Erasmus. During his stay in Leuven, he discovered a manuscript in the Park Abbey. It was written by the Italian humanist Lorenzo Valla, a strong advocate for using the philological approach to theology. According to Valla, the manuscripts handed down for the Vulgate, the Latin translation of the Bible, contained numerous errors and mistakes. Moreover, the Latin used was of questionable quality. In order to be *truly* able to understand the Bible, according to Valla – and Erasmus was his follower in this regard – an elementary knowledge of Latin was no longer enough: Greek and Hebrew were absolutely necessary as well. On top of that, a generous portion of textual criticism needed to be added, too.

↖ The Collegium Trilingue

In the years that followed, Erasmus stayed primarily in England and Italy, but he was back in Leuven in 1516. He was named councillor to the young emperor, Charles V. There he met up again with an old friend, Hieronymus Busleyden, with whom he had studied in Orléans. When Busleyden suddenly died in 1517, it turned out he had stipulated in his will that a new college was to be established within Leuven's university, one where three professors for Latin, Greek, and Hebrew, respectively, would be appointed. Erasmus took the practical execution of the will upon himself.

His initiative did not quite sit well with the theologians at Leuven. They held on to their Vulgate tightly, fearing that a critical study of the Bible would play into the hands of reformist theologians. The recent uproar around Martin Luther's *Ninety-Five Theses* was grist for the mill of the new college's opponents. Likely incited by these professors, protests also came from the students, although the scope of their demonstrations is difficult to determine. Even so, the Collegium Trilingue could count on powerful protectors, such as Utrecht's Cardinal Adrian (the future Pope Adrian VI, founder of the Pope's College), as well as William II de Croÿ, one of the most influential political figures at the court of Emperor Charles. In 1520, the college was definitively incorporated into the university.

Language instruction immediately experienced great success. In its first years, already around two hundred students – approximately ten percent of the entire student population – were taking classes there. After four years, the assembly hall with seating for 300 audience members had to be doubled in size, and even that expansion was not enough to handle the enormous influx. Thanks to the Collegium Trilingue, Leuven became a focal point for learning. Students from all over Europe came to Leuven, and alumni of the Collegium Trilingue spread the "Leuven method," as it was called, far beyond the boundaries of countries. Similar institutions were soon established in other university towns, though the network formed around Leuven's Collegium Trilingue would

Portrait of Erasmus of Rotterdam by Albrecht Dürer (1526).

continue to make up the core of the humanistic movement for a long time.

Student enthusiasm for studying languages is not the only explanation for this success. In and around the Collegium Trilingue, an atmosphere of innovation and discovery prevailed. The study of these ancient languages opened the door to the many unknown, mostly Greek treatises of classical authors. Texts from antiquity finally gave up their secrets. Accurately reading manuscripts and printed editions brought to light errors in copying or mistakes in interpretation. Traditional views had to be adjusted. Concluded debates could be taken up again. And that revision was not limited to disputes in theology, jurisprudence, or philosophy. Even in medicine and the natural sciences, philological criticism found avid adherents.

Among them, the most famous was the future anatomist Andreas Vesalius, at that moment still a philosophy student in the Faculty of Arts. Opinions are divided over his linguistic knowledge, although Vesalius clearly liked to show off his humanistic education. The renowned introductory chapter in his magnum opus – *De humani corporis fabrica*, in which he argued for reforms in medicine – was written in a Latin that was stilted and unnecessarily complicated. In the same work, he also provided Hebrew translations of anatomical body parts, possibly because he (like many of his colleagues) assumed that the authoritative Arabic treatises on medicine were written in Hebrew script. In many cases, however, Vesalius's Hebrew terms are written incorrectly, based more on their phonetic sound than on the grammatical structure of the words.

And yet, his humanistic use of language was more than just a superficial veneer. An important aspect of his work consisted of translating and studying ancient Greek texts. After studying philosophy in Leuven, Vesalius went to Paris, where he would study medicine under Johann Winter (or Guinter) von Andernach, himself an alumnus of Leuven's Collegium Trilingue and a personal friend of Erasmus. Winter was an expert in Greek medical treatises, which he translated and published. Under Winter, Vesalius became fascinated in the oeuvre of the Greco-Roman physician Galen. During Vesalius's stay in Paris, Winter was working on a translation of Galen's *Anatomices institutiones* (*Anatomical Institutions*). In order to better understand Galen's terminology, he carried out his own anatomical dissections. Vesalius assisted him in doing so, thus taking his first steps in anatomy.

When he was later tasked with anatomical dissections in Padua, Vesalius published a revised version of Winter's translation, in which he gave the first indications of his talent.

He pointed out the numerous errors or inconsistencies in Galen's work. They resulted, Vesalius supposed, from Galen conducting dissections primarily on animals and, as a result, drawing unjustified conclusions for human anatomy. Vesalius set about working on an anatomical description of the human body, based exclusively on dissections of human corpses, which resulted in his renowned *De Humani Corporis Fabrica* (*On the Fabric of the Human Body*). Despite the revolutionary character of this work, Vesalius saw it as a continuation or completion of Galen's vision, entirely in agreement with humanistic ideals.

Another alumnus of the Collegium Trilingue was the botanist Rembert Dodoens. Dodoens was only thirteen when he enrolled at Leuven in 1530. Before then, he had already studied Latin and Greek under Franciscus Hoverius, an alumnus of the Collegium Trilingue. Dodoens also took courses at the Collegium Trilingue in Leuven, in addition to studying medicine. It is possible – though uncertain – that he went on a few trips around Europe after graduating. Yet in 1542 he did publish, with Melchior Novesianus, an amended translation from the book about fevers written by the Byzantine physician Paulus Aeginetas, who was seen as one of the best experts on Galen's work. Dodoens based his rewrite on the original translation by Winter, though it is not known if he also met Winter personally. What is possible – though, again, not entirely certain – is that Dodoens also took care of the Dutch translation for Leonhart Fuchs's herbal titled *De historia stirpium* ([*Notable Commentaries*] *on the History of Plants*), published in Basel. The book constituted a milestone in European botany and became an icon for humanistic science. Fuchs argued for a return to the scientific concepts of the classical authors Dioscorides, Hippocrates, and Galen. *Den nieuwen Herbarius* (The New Herbal), as the Dutch translation was titled, marked the beginning of Dodoens's epoch-making botanical work.

Around the same time as Vesalius and Dodoens, Gemma Frisius was also studying at the Collegium Trilingue. Although he had graduated as a physician and had a medical practice, he was primarily known as a mathematician and cosmographer. By the age of twenty-one, he had already published a reprint of the introduction to cosmography by the German geographer Petrus Apianus. Frisius's edition experienced great success: there were no fewer than thirty of them, including translations into Dutch, French, and Spanish. The book contained more than just Apianus's writing, as Gemma added new texts. In one of them he laid out a new cartographical technique, now known as the triangulation method. It became the scientific basis for today's cartography.

Gemma is a pivotal figure for the Leuven Renaissance in scientific thought. Along with Hieremias Thriverius – again an alumnus of the Collegium Trilingue and author of numerous translations of and commentaries on Hippocrates and Galen – Gemma was present for the birth of the reformation of medical instruction at Leuven. Gemma helped Vesalius with the (not entirely legal) activity of taking a corpse from Leuven's gallows field. Gemma himself may have also taught anatomy at Leuven, though it is not clear whether he had an official appointment from the university. His knowledge of cosmography put him in touch with scholarly circles in Poland, informing him of Copernicus's new view of the world – long before Copernicus would publish anything on it. Gemma was enthusiastic. In a letter he expressed his expectation that Copernicus would usher in "a new earth, a new heaven, and a new world."[2] For Gemma, it was not so much a matter of Copernicus's new, heliocentric worldview

Portrait of Gemma Frisius by Jan van Stalburch (Leuven, 1557).

as it was about correcting antiquity's calculation methods for astronomy.

Students from home and abroad sought out Gemma for his mathematical expertise. With Gemma's support, the Dutchman Antonius Gogava translated Ptolemeus's *Tetrabiblos*, a key work in ancient astrology which enjoyed much esteem in the sixteenth century. For many years, the English mathematician John Dee studied with Gemma Frisius in Leuven, and befriended another student of Gemma (as well as an alumnus of the Collegium Trilingue): Gerard Mercator. Gemma was producing maps, globes, and mathematical instruments with Mercator even before Mercator established himself independently and set up his own shop.

The Collegium Trilingue is the crucial element connecting the lives and careers of Leuven's humanists. Even though the distance between language study and the natural sciences may seem very great, it turns out to be the spirit of critical investigation and direct contact with empirical sources (ranging from Greek manuscripts to anatomical dissections) that found adherents across any and all disciplinary borders. The Collegium Trilingue constituted a close-knit network of professors and students, book dealers and printers, humanistic scholars and scholarly humanists. Given its multifaceted character and its vigorous dynamic, it can be considered Leuven's first laboratory for learning.

STOP NO. 1 – COLLEGIUM TRILINGUE

Not much remains of the college that once made Leuven University famous. On the square known as the Vismarkt, the small alley Busleidengang commemorates the founder of the college. The passage leads to an inner courtyard where some remnants of the building are still visible. Most parts of the college have disappeared, however, razed or replaced by workers' quarters and artisans' shops. The name of the college lives on in a restaurant housed in the old buildings there and called: De 3 Tonghen (The 3 Tongues).

Initially, when the Collegium Trilingue was established, an existing location was sought out, but attempts to accommodate it in the St. Donatianus College (now gone) or Arras College (in the Naamsestraat) came to a dead end. To get things going as quickly as possible, though, a building complex on the Vismarkt was acquired. This ensemble of residential and service buildings, along with annexes, was the property of Professor Wouter de Leeuwe (a.k.a. Walterus Beka). He himself had acquired it from Bartholomeus de Madea, an Italian businessman who had set up a money-changing bureau and trade agency there.

The complex was located between the Vismarkt, the Augustijnenstraat, the Schrijnmakersstraat, and the former Scipstraat (now the Mechelsestraat). The college was accessible from each of these streets. Immediately after purchasing the complex, reconstruction work began. The former 'wine chamber' was transformed into a lecture hall, while the second floor had a number of rooms and a dormitory. Professor Beka's former residence housed a library, a dining hall, and rooms for the staff. The 'transversal' ('*dweershuis*') – a building opening out onto the courtyard – was set up as the president's residence. The college also had a large garden.

Over the years, additional modifications were carried out. The purchase of adjacent premises on the Mechelsestraat made the expansion of the lecture hall possible. In addition, a new, impressive gatehouse appeared on the Mechelsestraat, which would serve as the main entrance for the college.

During the eighteenth century, the heydays of the college were definitively behind it, which had financial effects as well. The buildings located on the Schrijnmakersstraat were sold and replaced by an inn called "Inde Drij Coppen" (In the Three Cups). The gatehouse on the Mechelsestraat also had to make way for the construction of a rental building (at the location of no. 34). By the end of the eighteenth century, only the wing for the lecture hall had retained its original role.

After the university was abolished under the French revolutionary regime, the college was sold to private individuals in 1806. In 1973, an attempt by the university to renovate the site could not be carried out. Only at the end of the twentieth century were various buildings gradually renovated.

Today, a number of architectural elements are still visible. Walking in by way of the Busleidengang, you come out onto a small inner courtyard. To your left is the 'transversal' with a structure spanning the passage and connecting to the building on the right. Straight ahead, the lecture hall wing is still visible. Although the façade shows quite a number of modifications, the building has retained its original supporting structure, including mostly original trusswork for the roof. To the right, you can still see traces of Professor Walterus Beka's residence.

GERARD MERCATOR: HUMANISM AND SCIENCE

Sixteenth-century humanism is often seen as a return to the culture of classical antiquity. Humanists rejected the medieval treatises that were, according to them, based on a textual transmission that was rarely reliable. In making the languages of classical antiquity their own, humanists strove for not only a re-sourcing of erudition, but also moral emancipation. A mind that managed to free itself from medieval conceptual frameworks would be able to develop more fully, as well as be inspired by the grand ideas of Ancient Rome.

What role did the natural sciences play in this regard? It is now generally accepted that the work of the major sixteenth-century scientific pioneers, like Andreas Vesalius and Nicolaus Copernicus, was just as much an homage to the work of their illustrious predecessors as it was a revolutionary break with the past. Was their humanism more than just a superficial veneer, though, a tribute to the culture of the era in which they lived? What are we to understand by humanistic science?

There is no one clear definition of humanistic science, just as humanism itself had a different concrete meaning for everyone. For some, the study of language constituted the core of the entire movement; for others, it involved the content of the texts being studied or a new openness in dealing with the world. In Leuven, this complexity of humanistic science was best embodied by Gerard Mercator. Although his name became a byword in cartography, the manner in which he did science was a combination of classical humanism and artisanal entrepreneurship.

The Mercator projection is a technique for laying out the curved surface of the earth on a flat map. The essential characteristic of this projection is such that when a ship travels a consistent course in a certain direction, the route can be marked out as a straight line on the Mercator map. For navigating the seas, the Mercator projection was an enormous aid, even though it would not prove so until much later. For Mercator himself, his famous method of projection was only one component of an especially ambitious lifework in which he placed time and space, humankind and the cosmos, the New and the Old World into a unified, overarching perspective.

Initially, Mercator's grand ideas did not seem to fit well in the academic straitjacket of the university. In 1532, greatly dissatisfied, Mercator left Leuven. He had just finished his philosophy studies in the Faculty of Arts, yet had come to determine that Aristotelian natural philosophy could not offer him any answers about the origin and the significance of the cosmos. For a few years, Mercator stayed in Antwerp and Mechelen. There he came into contact with cosmography, which was almost a complete revelation to him. Hij returned to Leuven and went to study with Gemma Frisius, who at that moment was already a European authority in the field of cosmography.

Cosmography studied the entirety of heaven and earth and what connected them both to each other. Its point of

Portrait of Gerard Mercator by Frans Hogenberg (1574).

In Effigiem carmen.

GErardus Mercator erat ſic cognitus orbi,
Duysburgi raperet cum fera parca virum.
Ottonos decies, binosq; exegerat annos
Et menſes octo, tresq; nouemq; dies.
Doctus erat verè, pius, integer, omnibus æquus,
Ingenio dexter, dexter & ipſe manu.
Sidera cum terris coniunxit, ſacra prophanis
Addidit, at rectè fecit vtrumq; tamen.
Aſtra Mathematicus radio deſcripſit acuto,
Et dedit in paruo conſpicienda globo.
In tabulas terræ ſpacioſum contulit orbem,
Inq; globo mundi regna videnda dedit.
Et ne quid cœli ſtudijs terræq; deeſſet,
Hiſtoriam docuit tempora certa loqui.
Sacraq; detexit vatum myſteria, Chriſti
Præcones iuſſit quattuor ire ſimul.
Atq; ea ſic fecit ſuperos vt vinceret omnes
Artifices, proprio marte, manuq; ſua.
Fœlix prole ſua, natisq; nepotibus ex ſe,
Spem gratæ certam poſteritatis habet.
At quod Chriſte tuum ſectatus ouile, beatus
Perpetuo tecum paſcua læta capit.
Et quamuis placuiſſe Duci non infima laus ſit,
Attamen eſt maior laus placuiſſe Deo.

Beneuolentiæ ergo Bernardus Furmerius Leouardienſis
Licentiatus iuris, mœſtus ſcribebat.

departure was the *Geographia* by Ptolemy, who had thought up a mathematical system for longitudes and latitudes, so as to situate every location exactly. Cosmography, though, did not remain limited to cartography. In describing towns and peoples, it also concerned flora and fauna, history and local custom, mythology and even Biblical history. Cosmography was not mathematics so much as it was erudition, exotic imagery, and commercial usefulness. In an era that was marked by voyages of discovery and openness of mind, cosmography corresponded perfectly to the intellectual interests of the Western world.

What was it in cosmography that Mercator found so attractive? In the foreword of his *Atlas*, he shed some light on his lifelong fascination with it. "I have set this man Atlas, so notable for his erudition, humaneness, and wisdom as a model for my imitation, sofar as my genius and strength suffice, as I begin to contemplate cosmography as though in the lofty mirror of the mind, if by chance I may be able to uncover some truth in matters hitherto obscure, which you might bring to your studies of wisdom. And just as the cosmos contains the number, species, order, harmony, proportion, virtues, and effects of all things, even so, beginning from the creation, I shall enumerate all its parts and contemplate them naturally, as a methodical account demands, according to the order of their creation, so that the causes shall be evident."[3]

For Mercator, cosmography was nothing less than the key to the essence of God's creation. In all of his work he looked for possibilities to bring together as much information as possible in meaningful overviews. His first map was one of the Holy Land, with a detailed rendering of all the places that, according to the Bible, the Jewish people had passed on their way to the Promised Land. Mercator developed his own system for putting the most information possible on maps. Even the cursive form of the letters used was not left to chance. Later in his career (at the time, he had moved to Duisburg), he also published a general chronology of world history as well as an edition comparing the four texts of the Gospel. The renowned world map from 1569 and his posthumously published *Atlas*

(1595) are other examples of how he ordered information into a systematic overview.

The science that Mercator envisioned had a moral significance. “From these [i.e., the knowledge of these causes],” he wrote, “comes science, and from science wisdom, which directs all things to good ends.”[4] It was what Mercator had already been searching for during his Leuven period: science that could serve as a guideline for the major challenges of his era, a guideline that is underpinned rationally and which additionally testifies to personal engagement and aesthetic design. Together, these elements characterize his works as humanistic. It is, however, also precisely these elements that were pushed aside by subsequent generations of scientists. After Mercator, science evolved more and more into an ideal of practical knowledge inspired by technology and trades. At the end of the sixteenth century, along with Mercator, humanistic science died a quiet death.

STOP NO. 2

VICUS ARTIUM

→ M Leuven, Leopold Vanderkelenstraat 28

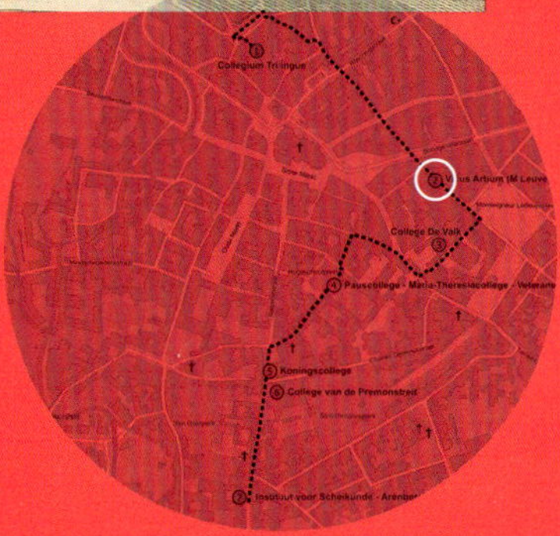

THE SCIENTIFIC REVOLUTION IN LEUVEN

In the history of science, the period between around 1550 and 1750 is referred to as the Scientific Revolution. At that point in time, Aristotelian natural philosophy was definitively pushed aside and replaced by a mechanistic conception of nature. Nature had to be investigated using mathematics and experimentation. Cause and effect were understood exclusively as the interaction between mechanical forces. The Scientific Revolution has also been described as the mechanization of our view of the world.

Quite a lot of ink has been spilled about the role of universities in this revolution. According to some, universities constituted the bulwark of traditional scholarship, and they had no part in the rise of the new science. The intellectual profile of the university was primarily defined by elite educational programs in theology and law, and such coursework was inclined more toward a status quo. Then again, others point out the role of the universities in confronting the old with the new. Even though the new science came about in the setting of artisanal trades, military applications, and commercial organizations, it was still academically trained scholars who extended its outcomes to the debate about the nature of knowledge and view of the world. In other words: without universities there would have been no talk of something like a 'scientific method,' and the new science could not have permeated the intellectual and social elites as quickly.

Leuven's university, too, was caught up in the maelstrom of the Scientific Revolution. Officially, it was said that Leuven professors remained loyal to the traditional orthodoxy. Teaching at De Valk 'pedagogy' (i.e., a residential college), the philosophy professor Libertus Fromondus can be considered a typical example. Initially, he was influenced by the groundbreaking astronomical observations of Galileo,

The Vicus Artium after its renovation in 1766.

but after Galileo's condemnation by the Church in 1633, he became a staunch opponent of the new natural science. When René Descartes sent him his *Discours de la Méthode* (1637) – indicating how much he valued the opinion of the Leuven professor – Fromondus rejected Cartesian philosophy as "excessively crass and mechanical."[5] Descartes had, after all, taken as his point of departure a worldview in which all natural phenomena, including all living creatures – except human beings – should be understood as machines. In 1662, the Faculty of Theology condemned Cartesian philosophy. And again, in 1695, a philosophy professor was called on the carpet because he had his students defend Cartesian theses.

In reality – despite resistance from theologians – Descartes's natural science had been integrated into the curriculum rather early on. Examining students' notebooks shows that the educational program was thoroughly revamped around 1658, and that Cartesian natural science was treated on equal footing with Aristotelian theories. In 1673, an inspection of the compliance with official regulations determined that Descartes's natural science was indeed being taught. During that audit, professors had apparently wanted to give the impression in particular that they continued to satisfy all the rules. "Nobody admits to wanting to teach Descartes," the findings read. "They say that they've taken up only a few mechanical explanations from his work." The inspector, however, was not going to be misled. "In effect," he concluded, "many professors are following Descartes's teaching."[6] Historical research has gone even further, showing that actually, around the time of the report,

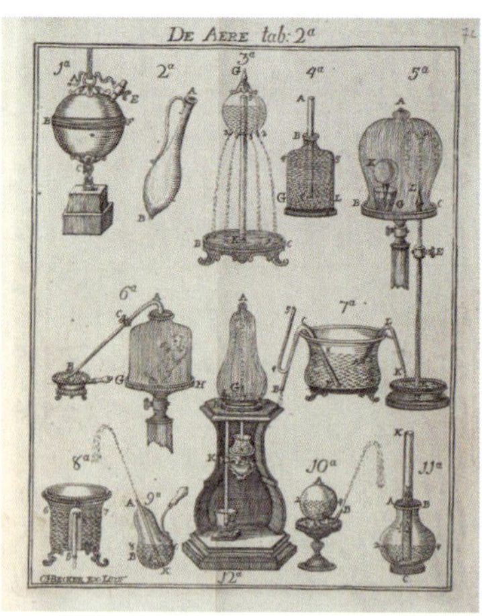

Engraving with various types of vacuum pumps. From an anonymous Leuven course notebook, titled *Tractatus de Aere* (second half of the eighteenth century).

hardly anyone could be found in Leuven who was not teaching Cartesian natural science.

Indeed, it was really about Cartesian *natural science*, not Cartesian philosophy. Descartes's doubts about method – with its renowned adage, "I think, therefore I am" – found a lot fewer adherents. Central to Cartesian natural science was the experiment. Although the mechanical groundwork for Cartesian thought was laid down with metaphysical arguments, the individuals interested in it were primarily seduced by the many demonstration experiments that supposedly proved the correctness of Descartes's scientific explanations. Not surprisingly, it was the Cartesian experiments especially – not so much Descartes's metaphysical theory – that found a place in instruction at Leuven.

In 1650, Arnold Geulincx had already pleaded for reforming how the university taught philosophy. In a public address, he argued that "a university's equipment can no longer consist of those fat books, full of fallacious reasoning, in which the blind talk about colors, and through which students lose their way, like a herd of cattle, in the opinions of the Ancients; instead, it comprises telescopes that bring the farthest removed phenomena in heaven closer. [...] Furthermore, botanical gardens and orchards, distillation flasks, furnaces, and magnets – in short, those things in which nature has stashed her wonders, and through which she can be approached and studied."[7]

A few years later, the instructional colleges of the Faculty of Arts began collecting scientific instruments. In 1669, the philosophy students of De Valk 'pedagogy' gave a number of 'mathematical and hydragogical [i.e., water-conveying] instruments' to their college. We know from students' course notes that the operation of a *vas pneumaticum* (a rudimentary vacuum pump) was explained around 1685. Around 1700, Professor Martinus van Velden had a Leeuwenhoek microscope that he showed to his students.

A 1755 inventory of all scientific instruments in the Faculty found that most of them were made "de la main de bons maitres"[8] (by the hand of good masters), but that they were outdated and sometimes in poor condition as well. The most frequently mentioned instruments had to do with optics and pneumatics (including a vacuum pump), but there were also instruments used for astronomy, mathematics, magnetism, and investigating electric phenomena. Notably, there is an absence of measuring instruments, like the thermometer and the barometer, which were nonetheless talked about in lecture notes.

Unfortunately, we do not know what instruction in experimental physics looked like. Nor do we know who was responsible for maintaining the instruments, or who among the professors was well versed enough to conduct the experiments. The Faculty recognized the difficulties in any case. In 1743, it requested financial support from the Austrian Habsburg government at that time, in order to purchase new instruments, though that request was refused. In 1754, Charles of Lorraine – then-governor of the Austrian Netherlands – decided that the Faculty of Arts had to sell all 'superfluous' books from its library, so as to purchase new instruments. The Faculty reacted with discontent. In the end, a compromise was reached: the government paid a considerable sum for the repair and purchase of instruments, whereas the Faculty committed to working out a modified curriculum. On March 17, 1755, a *Scola experimentalis* – a School for Experimental Physics – was established. The collection of instruments was housed in the Faculty's central *Vicus*, an estate used for lectures where demonstrations also took place.

The classes in experimental physics were given during the last two months of the two-year curriculum of the Faculty of Arts, possibly to encourage students to go through the entire curriculum until the very end. After all, quite a lot of students dropped out before the really tough final exams, which in theory, though not in practice, were required to continue studying in the higher faculties. The program for experiments was quite extensive and involved the entire *Physica* curriculum. Major topics were the divisibility and porosity of matter, gravity, vacuity, light and heat, electricity and magnetism.

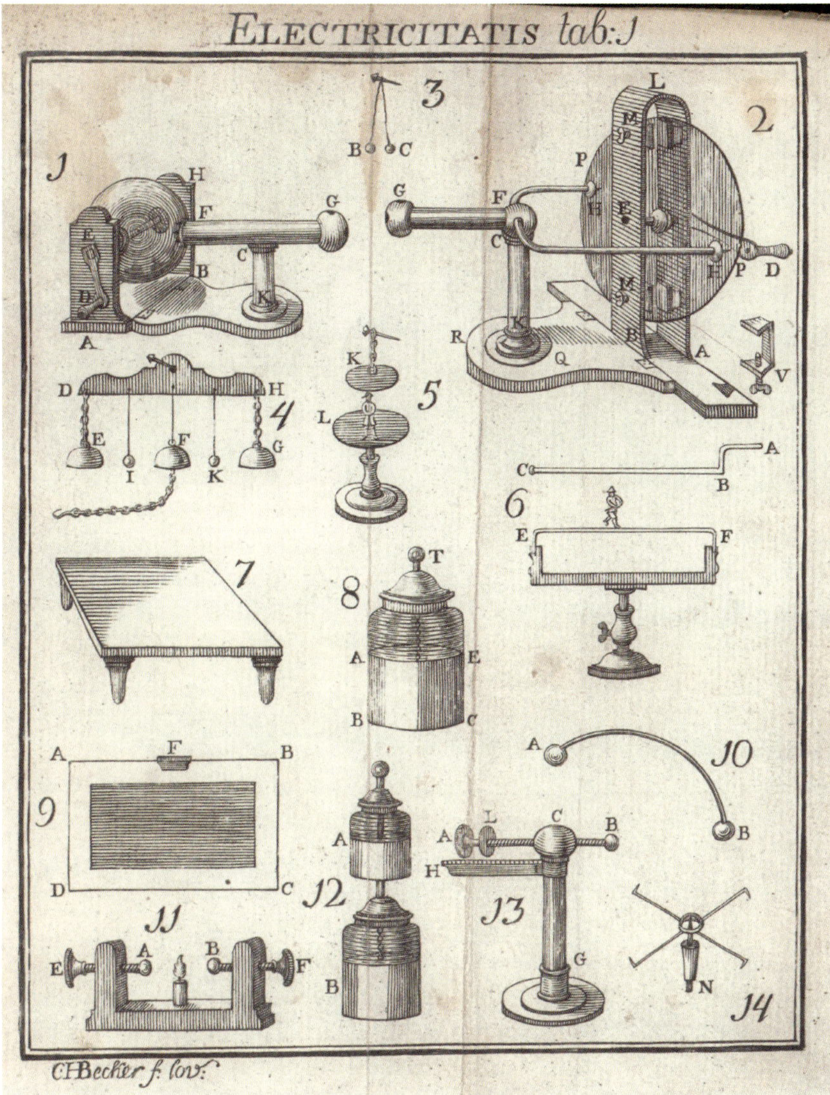

Engraving with an electrostatic machine and setups for electric experiments. From the course notebook *Physica*, written by Petrus Franciscus Van Audenrode (1785).

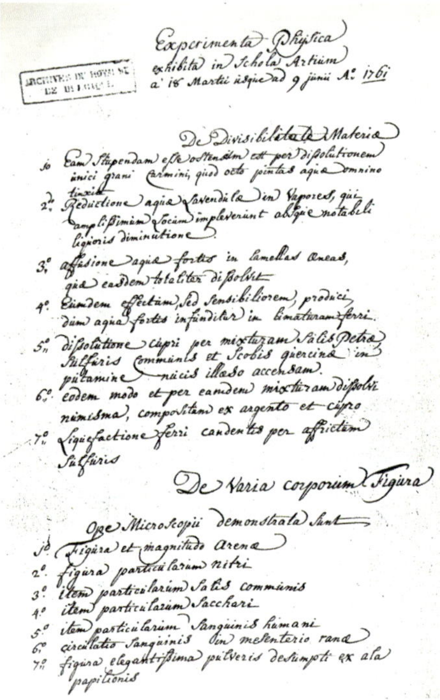

Experimenta Physica
exhibita in Schola Artium
a' 18 Martii usque ad 9 junii A° 1761

De Divisibilitate Materiae

De Varia corporum Figura

List of the experiments that were demonstrated in the Vicus Artium during the 1761 academic year.

And yet, the teaching was not successful. An English scholar visiting the school was devastating: the collection of instruments was composed "without knowledge, tast[e], order, or principles [...] more because they strike the senses, than the understanding."[9] Even the faculty determined that the maintenance of the instruments left a lot to be desired. Among the reasons given was the fact that the experiments were carried out by the Faculty's youngest professors, who did not have enough expertise and experience to operate the instruments properly. What ought to have been the Faculty's showcase for modern science turned out to be a reason for major concern after barely fifteen years.

A definitive solution came about when Jan Frans Thysbaert was named director of the School in 1771. Thysbaert was a theologian but after his studies he returned as a professor to the Faculty of Arts. In an ode dedicated to him a few years later, he was praised as "magno Neutoni compar,"[10] the equal of the great Newton. Thysbaert put things in order right away. He had defective instruments repaired and purchased dozens of new instruments from internationally renowned makers. To pay for all of it, Thysbaert negotiated a financial subsidy for the Faculty, and he gave up the income from the sale of his textbooks to the School. Now and then the School received donations as well. The duke of Arenberg donated a model of a steam engine. Emperor Joseph II, who visited the university in 1781, donated about two dozen natural history specimens from the estate of Charles of Lorraine.

Under Thysbaert, the School came to flourish. Foreign visitors were full of praise both for the School and for Thysbaert. The Dutchman Martinus van Marum wrote: "The Vicum is a college of the University, where physics instruments are collected. This collection, placed in various chambers, is rather significant. The superintendent, Mr. Canonicus Thysbaart, is a very knowledgeable man, who also makes new implements himself."[11] Van Marum mentioned that the same college had also assembled a natural history collection, including a number of fossils from Maastricht.

A premature end came to the School, however. In 1788, the Austrian Habsburg government decided that the thoroughly revamped university should be transferred to Brussels. More than a hundred wagons with furniture, books, and objects from the scientific collection were taken away. Yet as a result of the Brabant Revolution (1789–1790), the establishment of the university in Brussels was obstructed. Quite a lot of objects came back to Leuven. Thysbaert, who had been highly involved in establishing the new university, was no longer welcome. These were turbulent political times. After the French revolutionary army drove out the Austrians, the university was abolished in 1797. Once again, a few dozen crates with instruments were brought to Brussels. During the nineteenth century, there were still objects from Leuven's collections present in Brussels's Museum voor Kunst en Vlijt (Museum for Art and Industry), but none of them returned to Leuven.

STOP NO. 2 – VICUS ARTIUM

Among the oldest buildings belonging to the university is the Vicus Artium, the 'estate of the arts.' This formerly private residence was purchased on April 30, 1426, for teaching philosophy in the Faculty of Arts. In the years that followed, however, instruction was shifted more and more to the four residential colleges (called: 'pedagogies'), where both students and professors stayed. As a result, the importance of the central Vicus decreased. By the end of the eighteenth century, only classes in ethics and rhetoric were held here. Every year in the Vicus, celebrations were also held for the *primus*, the student who ranked first in the Faculty's final exams. These comparative examinations were, by the way, unique in Europe. University exams were mostly conducted through public debates and examinations.

From 1755 forward, the School for Experimental Physics was housed in the Vicus. This initiative, which fit in well with the modernization policies of the Austrian Habsburg government, was backed up with a complete renovation of the building. Lauren-Benoît Dewez, the well-known neoclassical court architect, was called in for this project. In Leuven, Dewez had also been involved in the construction or renovation of the King's College, the gateway to the (old) Botanical Garden, and Vlierbeek Abbey. The Vicus Artium was equipped with an auditorium for physics demonstrations, along with various rooms for storing scientific instruments and the natural history collection.

After the university was abolished in 1797, the Vicus was used as a court of first instance (or trial court). During World War I, the building was pretty much entirely destroyed. Only the portico was preserved and integrated into the main entryway for the new municipal library. In 2004–2009, that building was torn down for the construction of the museum M Leuven. The portico for the Vicus Artium still forms the entry for the building behind it, which once again can be called the 'estate of the arts.'

The impressive gateway still contains a few references to the 'scientific' past of the building. On the base of the column to the left of the center passage, an inscription recalls when the first stone was laid for the new construction of the Vicus Artium on August 19, 1766, by Count Karl Johann Philipp von Cobenzl, the plenipotentiary minister of the Austrian Netherlands in Brussels. To the right of the closed passageway, there is a commemorative plaque mentioning both the former Faculty of Arts and the courthouse.

GERARD VAN GUTSCHOVEN AND THE SPREAD OF CARTESIANISM

For hundreds of years, Aristotelian natural philosophy constituted the dominant framework in which scientists thought about nature. For the most part, it was the work of the French philosopher René Descartes that ultimately brought an end to its dominance. He conceived a completely new worldview in which all phenomena were explained by the movement and force of extremely small particles of matter. The world was a machine. And he made an exception only for the human soul.

Descartes's theory ran into quite a lot of resistance among conservative scholars. The more resistance there was, however, the more intense the enthusiasm of proponents became. Cartesianism succeeded in definitively pushing Aristotle aside.

Leuven constituted one of the early mainstays in the spread of Cartesianism. Descartes himself sent his first book, *La Discours de la méthode*, to two internationally renowned Leuven professors: the professor of philosophy Libertus Fromondus and the professor of medicine Vopiscus Fortunatus Plempius. Descartes had gotten to know Plempius in Amsterdam. Undoubtedly, he was hoping for a positive response, but that did not happen. Both Fromondus and Plempius were extremely critical of Descartes. Through Fromondus's actions, Cartesianism was formally forbidden at the Faculty of Arts, though in practice more and more philosophy professors adopted Cartesian theses.

An avid proponent of Cartesianism in Leuven was the physician, anatomist, mathematician, and botanist Gerard van Gutschoven. Van Gutschoven was born in Leuven and had already obtained his medical degree at the age of twenty. He soon also demonstrated a talent for mathematics. He drafted an accurate map of the siege of Leuven by French and Dutch troops (1635), indicating the defense works around the town. A few years later we find him in Utrecht. Around that time, he met Descartes (who had settled in the Dutch Republic), and he may have even stayed with him for a time.

In 1644, he was back in Leuven. Two years later he was named holder of the royal professorship for mathematics. This professorship had been set up by the Spanish king to provide mathematical instruction for surveyors, cartographers, or navigation masters. We are not very well informed about Van Gutschoven's teaching. He published a few textbooks on building fortifications and calculating with logarithms, but we cannot rule out that he also taught new Cartesian mathematics (with Cartesian coordinates x, y, and z). Van Gutschoven was in contact with the major mathematicians of his era, like Christiaan Huygens, Andreas Tacquet, and René François de Sluse. Gutschoven's curve (or kappa curve) in algebra is named after him.

Van Gutschoven was a strong advocate for Cartesianism at the university. In part, that support happened indirectly via his brother Willem who, as a professor in the Faculty of Arts, had his students defending Cartesian theses very early on. More directly, Gerard engaged in various opportunities for spreading Descartes's work. That involvement became especially clear after he was named professor of anatomy in 1659. In the same year, he wrote a fiery critique of Plempius's renowned book about ophthalmology, in which Van Gutschoven laid out a Cartesian conception of the eye. Plempius himself

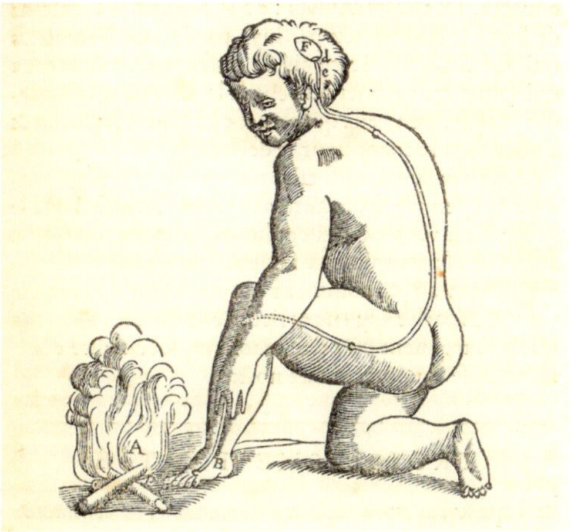

Illustration drawn by Gerard van Gutschoven for Descartes's *Traité de l'Homme* (1664).

published the critique in the third edition of his *Ophthalmographia*, including a reply, of course. Tensions between Plempius and Van Gutschoven remained, even in the years that followed.

Around the same time, Van Gutschoven was approached by the French philosopher Claude Clerselier who was engaged in publishing a posthumous work by Descartes, his *Traité de l'Homme* (*Treatise on Man*). Clerselier asked Van Gutschoven to draw the scientific illustrations for the text. Without those illustrations, after all, the text could not be properly read. The work was taking some time, such that Clerselier had meanwhile also received illustrations from two other scholars. Yet in the published edition, Clerselier would end up using pretty much all of Van Gutschoven's illustrations, which, according to him, were of a better quality.

Van Gutschoven was the personification of the modern Cartesian natural scientist. Just like Descartes, he was well grounded in mathematics, and he had enjoyed medical training as well. He was interested in the construction of lenses, built mathematical instruments, and investigated human anatomy from a mechanistic perspective. Van Gutschoven died unexpectedly, however, in 1668. By then, Cartesianism had already firmly ensconced itself in instruction at Leuven.

STOP NO. 3

DE VALK COLLEGE

→ Tiensestraat 41

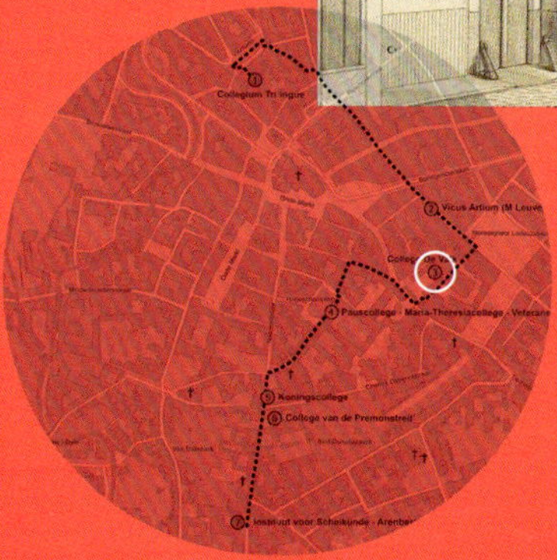

THE FIRST LABORATORIES

On the façade of the residential college called De Valk (the falcon), there is a commemorative plaque honoring Jan-Pieter Minckelers, who "discovered" coal gas "in this institute." The memorial site was inaugurated on September 4, 1948, by the Engineers' Union from the Special Schools of the Catholic University of Leuven. Coal gas, also known as light (or town) gas, was of great importance for nineteenth-century lighting and heating technology. The engineers wanted to highlight the discovery of their illustrious predecessor.

The homage to Minckelers was indeed justified, although De Valk was not the site where Minckelers carried out his investigation. It is more likely that it happened in the Vicus, where the School for Experimental Physics had its headquarters. Minckelers was a professor at De Valk residential college, but this college was not equipped for doing scientific research. (In 1627, students had caused a huge explosion in the building. Though the event was thought to have been an experiment gone out of control, it may instead have been merely a kind of – scientific – vandalism.)

College De Valk in the middle of the nineteenth century.

The location of the first laboratories is difficult to recover. Simple trial demonstrations could just be carried out in an auditorium. Yet for more complicated setups, especially chemical experiments, more was needed. Until the middle of the eighteenth century, the university in all likelihood did not have any room that could have been called a laboratory.

In the seventeenth century, the term "laboratory" was associated in the first place with workplaces for alchemists. Laboratories were dark, secluded chambers where the alchemist attempted to accelerate normal, naturally occurring processes in furnaces and distillation flasks. In this way, the goal was to transform matter into its most perfect form. Alchemy found applications in gold- and silversmith work, in preparing medicines, and in extracting mineral ores.

The belief that alchemists were able to turn metal into gold aroused enormous interest. Even university scholars engaged in alchemical investigations. Isaac Newton is known to have spent more time on alchemy than he did on his – nonetheless ground-breaking – work in physics.

In Leuven, (al-)chemical investigations appear to have been adopted in the academic program rather late. In the early seventeenth century, the Leuven alumnus Jan-Baptist van Helmont did work out an iatrochemical theory, in which chemical processes in the body were considered the cause of illnesses. Van Helmont, however, came into conflict with Leuven's theologians. Within the university, his theories would not be emulated.

Only in 1685 was a royal professorship for chemistry created at Leuven's Faculty of Medicine. The program concentrated primarily on preparing chemical medications. In view of the fact that the university considered setting up a chemistry lab to be too expensive, practical demonstrations took place at the professor's home. For professorial candidates, having your own laboratory was an important asset. In 1696, the Faculty explicitly took into account the presence of a private "laboratorium valde sumptuosum"[12] (a very well-equipped lab) in the case of one candidate.

The costs for making experiments ran very high, however. During the eighteenth century, it was not unusual for the chemistry professor to be appointed as well to professorships for anatomy and botany, so that he could supplement his relatively modest salary with extra income.

The most renowned chemistry professor in Leuven was Hendrik Jozef Rega. Admittedly, his appointment lasted only a little more than an academic year. His subsequent appointment (in anatomy) did not last long, either. His career really did not take off until 1719. In that year he obtained his doctorate in medicine, set up a flourishing medical practice, was named *professor primarius* in pathology, and was additionally appointed as the university's rector.

Rega provided the university with its first scientific laboratories. In 1738, he bought the university a manor house

Portrait, attributed to Anna Maria Blendeff, of a likely scholar at Leuven – possibly Hendrik Jozef Rega – with his library and a chemical distillation furnace (1721).

with annexes and an orangery in the Minderbroedersstraat, adjacent to Voer Creek. The estate, which had belonged to Michiel Van Ophem (a botany professor during his lifetime), was transformed into a botanical garden with new plantings. In 1744, Rega erected an anatomical theater on the corner of the property. At first, Van Ophem's former residence was rented out; afterwards, the academic press was housed there. Finally, from 1756 forward, a chemistry laboratory and a mineralogical collection were located there. In doing so, the university had an impressive and coherent ensemble of facilities for the various basic sciences for medicine.

In this regard, we do need to make a few side notes. For each of these basic sciences, a royal professorship was created. If we place the royal medical professorships (anatomy, botany, chemistry) alongside that of the Faculty of Arts (mathematics) and, moreover, add the particular efforts made by the Austrian Habsburg government for the School for Experimental Physics in the Vicus Artium, then it is clear how much pressure was applied by the political regime to integrate these basic sciences into the academic world at Leuven and, in this way, direct the orientation of university instruction. The university was glad to follow along, but instruction by the royal professors was not made compulsory in any part of the curriculum. Students were not given examinations about the content of these extra courses. The royal professors were not even authorized to act as examiners. Incidentally, their courses were directed not only toward philosophy or medical students, but toward non-academic professionals as well, like surgeons, surveyors, and apothecaries. The royal professors were clearly a rung lower on the academic ladder than the university professors, who also sat on the executive council of the Faculty.

Het Varken residential college (no longer extant) on the Hogeschoolplein. Colored drawing in the course notebook titled *Logica*, written by Joannes Wouters, 1648–1650.

The location of the Anatomical Theater, the Botanical Garden, and the chemistry laboratory in the Minderbroedersstraat is also quite relevant: they were all relatively far removed from the center of town. Classes in theory were still held in the University Hall, such that the students had to go quite a long way to take classes in the Minderbroedersstraat laboratories. The number of students taking chemistry classes, then, was very limited. The laboratory complex on the Minderbroedersstraat can almost be considered a second campus, which, as a result of its location, remained physically as well as mentally isolated from the heart of the university.

In that light, it is also important to mention that at the end of the eighteenth century, there was a certain rapprochement between the royal professors from the Faculty of Medicine and the philosophy professors who were also interested in the modern natural sciences. In 1783, the chemistry professor Van Bochaute lent his collaboration to the philosophy professors Thysbaert and Minckelers in their search for a gas that was lighter than air, and which could launch a hot-air balloon. Notably: the results of the chemistry professor turned out to be not as good as those of Minckelers, the philosophy professor. The discovery of coal gas, then, was legitimately attributed to Minckelers.

Various Leuven scientists met one another, too, in the Brussels Academy for Sciences, established in 1772, following the model of similar academies in other countries. Van Bochaute, in particular, was very active and sent in various treatises. He was perhaps also the first Leuven scientist to publish in an international journal, the French *Journal de physique*. Van Bochaute followed – as did Minckelers, incidentally – developments very closely in France, where Lavoisier was working on a new nomenclature for chemical substances. In 1787, Van Bochaute proposed a nomenclature of his own, based largely on the Greek names given by Lavoisier. His colleagues in the Academy at Brussels, however, found the nomenclature too cumbersome and unnecessarily complicated: *chrysos* for gold, *antroxe* for carbon dioxide, *oenophlogos* for alcohol. Wisely, Van Bochaute resigned himself to Lavoisier's system.

STOP NO. 3 – DE VALK COLLEGE

The De Valk College (Falcon College) is the only surviving example of the four residential colleges of the Faculty of Arts. In a residential college, students and teachers lived together, and instruction was given there, too. Initially, instruction in philosophy took place in the Vicus Artium, and the students lodged with burghers or professors in town. Because philosophy students were often very young – fourteen years old was no exception – the custom caught on more and more of bringing the students together in colleges, where they could be properly paid attention to. In the fifteenth century, four such colleges were officially recognized by the Faculty as instructional colleges. They were called 'pedagogies'. Each college bore the name of the building where they were originally located: *Porcus* (The Pig), *Lilium* (The Lily), *Castrum* (The Castle), and *Falco* (The Falcon).

There was healthy competition between these pedagogies. During final exams, the best students from each pedagogy took on one another in public debates. The winner was lavishly honored as the *primus*, both at the university and in their hometown. A positive outcome on the final exams was an important asset for a continuing academic career.

The division of the Faculty into four pedagogies also allowed a certain degree of independence for each college in organizing instruction. In the seventeenth century, however, in order to retain some control, not only was the teaching material determined through joint consultation (the so-called *materiae promotionis*), but also the students were required to take notes on all the content of their classes. That is why course notes are also called dictations: the professor literally dictated the text, sometimes also in a Q&A format as preparation for the exams.

De Valk residential college was originally located in the Savoyestraat, yet moved to its present location in 1543. A description from that time talks about a complex with multiple buildings around a central inner courtyard with a four-story gatehouse. In the centuries that followed, the college was thoroughly rebuilt. Today's left wing, the rear annex, and the gateway were built in 1782–1783, in a monumental neoclassical style following a plan by the Leuven architect Claude Fisco. Among other works, Fisco also drafted the layout for the squares called the Martelaarsplein and the Nieuwe Graanmarkt in Brussels.

After the university was abolished, the De Valk College was used as a military hospital until the middle of the twentieth century. In 1866, a fire destroyed part of the building, and only the gatehouse was preserved. In 1873, the college was partially rebuilt, according to Fisco's plans. The original left wing was shortened, and the right wing was erected to be symmetrical with the left wing.

Since 1953, the building has once again been property of the university. The classrooms are used by the Faculty of Law.

JAN PIETER MINCKELERS: SCIENCE AND UTILITY

In a petition to Austrian Emperor Francis II of Habsburg-Lorraine, Jan-Pieter Minckelers briefly summed up his career at Leuven: "I didn't enter into offers for easier, more lucrative appointments at the university, which the theologians repeatedly promised me at that time; I chose instead to make myself useful in my teaching, and that's why I dedicated myself fully to studying philosophy. I have especially devoted myself to the study of physics, with all the zeal that the love for this profession can awaken in someone."[13]

Minckelers had come to Leuven in 1764, at the age of sixteen. After studying philosophy at the De Valk College, he studied theology and was ordained as a sub-deacon in 1770 (and as a deacon, later on). The next year he was named *professor secundarius* at his former residential college. Traditionally, an appointment as *secundarius* was only temporary, either because the instructor was at the same time finishing his studies at a higher institution and would leave the university afterward, or because he took over a *primarius* position that had been vacated. Minckelers's career was atypical: he did not become *secundarius* until after he had ended his studies in theology, and he never became *primarius*. It may, as he wrote, have had something to do with his love for experimental physics. Normally the *primarius* taught the more theoretical subjects, whereas the *secundarius* took on the ones more oriented toward practical experience.

In his petition to the emperor, Minckelers also mentioned that he had redesigned most of the courses about the natural sciences for the Faculty of Arts. In the Minckelers archives, preserved at the university in Liège, there are manuscripts that confirm his claim. In particular, he closely attended to discoveries and theories in chemistry which were making the rounds in France and England. The 1783 discovery of coal gas was no stroke of luck: Minckelers had been intensively involved with chemical research since at least 1778.

During Minckelers's stay at Leuven, the university was undergoing profound changes. Initial reforms of the curriculum took place in 1764. A complete overhaul of the old university structures and privileges would be implemented in the 1780s, including – as its dramatic climax – the transfer of the university to Brussels (preferably labelled as founding a new university under state supervision). This final act was quickly undone by the Brabant Revolution, but the glory of the Old University at Leuven was never entirely restored. In 1797, it was abolished by the French revolutionary regime.

During the reform movement, the natural sciences played a prominent role. According to the Austrian Habsburg authorities, they constituted the showcase for a modern university that kept up with its times. The increasing pressure on the university to adapt was framed within a wider range of reforms that were imposed by Joseph II on the Austrian Netherlands. Minckelers was a great proponent of this modernization at the university.

Why was so much attention paid to the natural sciences in this regard? From today's vantage point, it may seem self-evident, but in the eighteenth century that was not at

Commemorative plaque for Jan-Pieter Minckelers, mounted on the façade of De Valk College.

all the case. Universities were not training institutes for physicists or chemists – professions that did not even exist at all at that time. The entire university curriculum revolved around educating an elite social class that found positions in the Church, the State, or healthcare. In this regard, the natural sciences played a subordinate role. Chemistry and botany were taught at the Faculty of Medicine, but they were limited to the preparation of medications. What could an electrostatic machine contribute to the education of theologians or jurists?

The key to understanding the eighteenth-century enthusiasm is the word "utility." With the reforms in the curriculum at the Faculty of Arts in 1764, the school had already indicated that it wanted to expand the program of instruction with a "quantité de choses aussi utiles qu'agréables"[14] (number of subjects both useful and delightful). Nearly identical wording is found in a report by a professor from Strasbourg, who came to assess the level of the university at Leuven, on behalf of the Austrian Habsburg authorities: the university was in decline, the instruction concentrated too much on empty phrases and scholastic subtleties. Providing new course content was urgently needed; he explicitly named geography and history, "parties utiles et agréables qu'on devrait joindre aux tristes études de la grammaire, des vocabulaires, phraséologies et autres minuties scolastiques"[15] (useful and delightful components that ought to be attached to the dreary study of grammar, vocabulary, syntax, and other scholastic minutiae). In Brussels in 1769, as part of the large-scale reforms of intellectual life in the Austrian Netherlands, a *Société littéraire* was created, predecessor to the aforementioned Academy and oriented toward "les sciences utiles à l'humanité et nécessaires à l'industrie" (sciences useful for humanity and necessary for industry).[16]

The 'royal' laboratories of the Old University: the Anatomical Theater, the entrance gate to the Botanical Garden, and the chemistry laboratory.

The interest in the natural sciences was part of a broader social appreciation for useful knowledge. In his 1758 *Manuel physique*, a French author wrote: "Le goût de la Physique est aujourd'hui si répandu dans le monde, qu'il semble nécessaire, pour s'y produire avec honneur, d'en avoir au moins une teinture"[17] (The taste for Physics today is so widespread in the world that for a person to present himself honorably it seems necessary to have at least a hint of it). The natural sciences were a form of urbane snobbery, a kind of social capital that could be deployed in elite salons, an ornament of worldly, civilized culture. The natural sciences were 'useful' because, in contrast to philosophical and literary debates, they were not about politics and religion, but about the choice of fertilizer, the dangers of earthquakes, or the economic usefulness of exotic crops.

For Minckelers, 'utility' had, above all, the meaning of practicality. The discovery of coal gas came about following a request from the duke of Arenberg, who was looking for a way to fill a balloon with a gas lighter than air. Minckelers further discovered that this gas could also be used as a source for lighting. On special occasions, according to eyewitnesses, he lit his classroom (or the auditorium in the Vicus building?) with coal gas.

Minckelers, however, did not commercialize applications for gas lighting. Others after him did so, resulting in his part in the discovery getting somewhat lost in the background. From the middle of the nineteenth century forward, when the Industrial Revolution was inundating Europe, Belgian and Dutch scientists once again stood up for 'their' Minckelers. In 1904, in his hometown Maastricht, he got a statue with a gas torch that burns at scheduled intervals. In 1948, a statue of him was also erected in Heverlee by Leuven engineers. Minckelers is depicted on it together with the duke of Arenberg. Engineers understood very well that applied science was only possible given the financial support of an investor.

STOP NO. 4

POPE'S COLLEGE • MARIA-THERESIA COLLEGE • VETERANS' COLLEGE

→ Hogeschoolplein 3 (Pope's College) · Sint-Michielsstraat 2-6

OLD COLLEGES, NEW LABORATORIES

After the Old University was abolished, the colleges and the university's entire assets were seized by the French revolutionary regime. The colleges were sold to private individuals, or used as government buildings (courthouse, gendarmerie, prison, barracks, military hospital, etc.). In 1805, the remaining buildings were transferred to the municipal administration. Of these, the University Hall, the Pope's College, the Premonstratensian College, and the Anatomical Theater were allocated to the new State University in 1817.

Most of these buildings were erected or renovated in the last two decades of the eighteenth century and were in relatively good shape. Even so, as good as everything that the Old University had developed in scientific infrastructure completely disappeared. The chemistry lab in the Minderbroedersstraat was now used as a dissection hall and anatomical collection. The scientific instruments and natural history collections from the Vicus Artium (which was no longer part of the State University) had been taken away to Brussels. The old Botanical Garden could no longer be used.

A generous inaugural subsidy made it possible for university and town alike to develop new infrastructure. Professors were sent out to purchase the necessary scientific instruments. The State insisted on having the instruments manufactured by domestic instrument makers, in particular, but for important physics devices they still called upon renowned Parisian instrument makers. The Physics Institute (Kabinet van Natuurkunde) was housed in the Premonstratensian College.

In assembling the natural history collection, the university watched for public auctions of private collections. In this regard, too, specimens were acquired from beyond the country's borders. An 1828 description mentioned 128 mammals, 740 birds, 64 amphibians, 618 fish, 83 lizards

The Pope's College at the time of the State University (1830).

and turtles, 3100 insects, 895 shellfish, 1200 fossils, and 170 invertebrates. The collection of minerals counted no less than 10,000 specimens. Further, there were "several human skeletons and skulls" and 60 "complete skeletons of animals."[18] The entire collection was housed in the King's College.

The chemistry laboratory was located in the Veterans' College. It consisted of a number of furnaces, a few glass and porcelain receptacles, and additionally "a large galvanic trough apparatus for electricity, a hydraulic press by Réal, a large distillation structure, and a fine scale for weighing liquid." Accounts for the laboratory mention the Brussels druggists Delfosse and Vautier as suppliers, possibly for the necessary chemical products. The tools were made in 1820 by "the Vanderbuecken Brothers, machinists and gunmakers, at Loven (*sic*). [...] The copper products have been made by wid. Tossyn, and those in tin by Vanhool, both in this town." In 1824, an Amphitheatrum Chemicum was constructed with related cabinetry. The garden of the Veterans' College was used to grow medicinal plants for instructional purposes.

In 1819, a property between the Kapucijnenvoer and the Heilige Geeststraat was purchased for teaching botany. Here, in the following years, a splendid botanical garden with an orangery arose, as planned by Charles Vander Straeten, the royal architect. Ten years later, this Botanical Garden already counted more than 8,000 plants. The Botanical Garden was managed by the professor for botany but was also open to the public every afternoon.

Notably, all the scientific disciplines were at first brought together in one single faculty, the Faculty for Chemical and Physical Sciences. Each professor was responsible for one discipline. Most students took classes in the natural sciences as preparation for a medical (or possibly legal) education, but they could also graduate as a doctor in the sciences. They were able to distinguish themselves during their studies by taking part in annual inter-university contests. In this way, King William I's state universities laid the foundation for the scientific boom in Belgium after 1830.

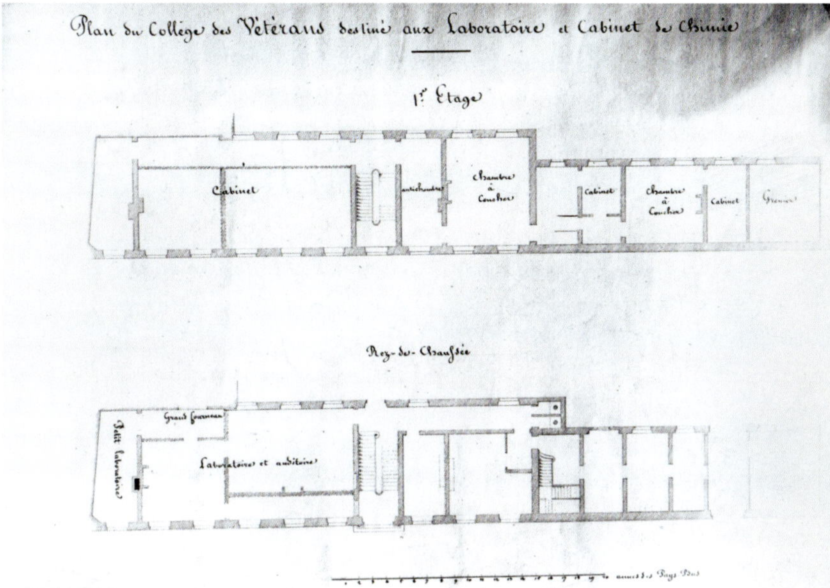

Installation of chemistry labs in the Veterans' College, ca. 1818.

The position of the faculties for the sciences was scaled back, however, after Belgian independence. In the 1835 legislation on higher education they once again, just as before, were given the role of preparatory faculties for advanced degrees. Courses of study were limited to the basic knowledge necessary; only in highly exceptional cases did a student follow a program that could lead to the doctoral degree. This subordinate role for natural sciences instruction worked out well for the Catholic University, which was established in Leuven starting in 1835. Continuing a separate faculty for the sciences was just enough for the Catholic institution to be able to take pride in the fact that it was not neglecting the rapid progress being made in the sciences, without needing to pay too much attention to scientific debates. Most of the science instructors at Leuven did not really stand out in producing original research.

Not surprisingly, the budgets for developing and maintaining the scientific collections and laboratories remained limited. Established within the framework for the freedom of instruction, the Catholic University could not count on subsidies from the State. It relied primarily on donations as well as the annual appeal made in churches. More often than not, the purchase of new specimens or apparatus had to paid for by the professors themselves.

In the last couple of decades of the nineteenth century, the Faculty entered an accelerated phase of rapid growth. In 1864, a Catholic engineering program was established at Leuven, which was added to the Faculty of Sciences. This event had major effects. From mere preparatory instruction, the program developed into a fully-fledged, four-year course of study. In ten years' time, the number of professors grew from six to seventeen, while the number of students doubled, even though there was no rush right away for the Catholic initiative (its diploma was not officially recognized by the Belgian state).

The university's Botanical Garden.

De Marbaix del. Serres du Jardin botanique de l'Univ.é de Louvain. Lemaître Lith. de Jobard

In the Maria-Theresia College, three new auditoriums and a large drafting room were installed. Space was also created for collections of industrial models and machines. Additionally, auxiliary laboratories were set up: a chemistry practice lab, as well as two labs for analytical and industrial chemistry, respectively.

A second, major change was the method of instruction that had come over from Germany, and in which students were engaged in independent research concerning current debates in their fields. In this so-called German model, laboratories played a central role. A university education could not consist of only theoretical coursework any longer. Students also had to be able to show competence in laboratory techniques and distinguish themselves through original work. As a result of the widely recognized, leading position of science in Germany, many countries adopted this German model. Laboratories became the showplace for the modern university.

The chemist Louis Henry promoted the German model at Leuven. After his studies, Henry had gone to Germany and had experienced the new approach there first-hand. Back in Leuven, he campaigned for reforms in scientific instruction. Indeed, in 1871, an ambitious program was announced, with six specializations for doctoral study. The reforms, however, attracted few students. Even when legislation provided for the introduction of practical labwork in 1876, Leuven only responded half-heartedly. As a private university, Leuven did not have the means to proceed with any major expansion of its laboratories. In 1881, the Faculty of Sciences sounded the alarm: "C'est la gène ici et là la misère"[19] (It's embarrassment here, and it's misery over there). Nothing changed much. In the years that followed, too, the initiative came primarily from individual professors, each one shaping the scientification of the Faculty in their own way.

The introduction of practical labwork in university instruction placed a heavy burden on the already precarious finances of the Catholic University. Building new laboratories at Leuven was ruled out. In the nineteenth century, the university did not have sufficient means to invest in new

Microscopy hall in the Carnoy Institute (Villers College).

buildings for scientific research. The liberal government conveniently made use of this situation by providing the state universities in Ghent and Liège with splendid 'palaces of science' during the heat of this battle between public and religious schools (the '*Schoolstrijd*'). In this way, the fight against Catholic Leuven was waged on the battlefield of science.

Laboratory instruction also affected the students' education. During a classic lecture, students listen passively to the instructor's presentation. In the laboratory, though, the instructor stands next to the student. They give directions and observe the progress of the student individually. Doing so, the students are not only judged on their knowledge, but also on their competence, inventiveness, and originality. The university was not only imparting knowledge to the student, but also a scientific, critical mindset.

Another result was the creation of research institutions. In the laboratory (the best) students got the opportunity to participate in the professor's research. In this way, the students became the master's disciples. In their subsequent careers they often continued the work of their mentor. It was not uncommon for the founder of the 'school' to become the object of veneration, to be commemorated in *Festschriften* and celebrations with great affection and respect by his students. Yet this situation also had a dampening effect: the dominant position of the professor made the introduction of new avenues for research more difficult.

From the end of the nineteenth century forward, laboratories had begun to spread out over Leuven's town center. In 1889, the Carnoy laboratory for microscopy moved from the Pope's College to the spacious, redesigned Villers College in the Vaartstraat (where the Justice of the Peace and the State Archives are now located). Ten years later, a new laboratory for bacteriology was built in the present Vital Decosterstraat (used now as the BAC ART LAB); a year later, the Institute for Electromechanics opened its doors in the Vlamingenstraat (now the Vlerick Leuven Management School); and in 1909, the Arenberg Institute was inaugurated as a brand new laboratory building for chemistry in the Naamsestraat (now known as the STUK Arts Center). After World War I, the gradual relocation of laboratories to suburban Heverlee was set in motion.

STOP NO. 4 – POPE'S COLLEGE · MARIA-THERESIA COLLEGE · VETERANS' COLLEGE

For those with a little bit of imagination, Leuven's square called the Hogeschoolplein offers a good idea of the impact of the university's colleges on the town's urban fabric. Some imagination is necessary, for in fact most of the colleges have by now disappeared.

In the middle of the square once stood Het Varken residential college, one of the four colleges of the Faculty of Arts. After the university was abolished in 1797, the building fell into decline. In 1806, at the initiative of the municipal government, it was razed to make way for a square. On the south side of the square, we can still see remnants of the adjacent Standonck College, which was partially sold to private individuals.

The largest college is the Pope's College, founded in 1523, as established in the last will and testament of Adrianus Floriszoon Boeyens. He was once professor and rector at Leuven, but since 1522, after a remarkable career in the Church, he had become Pope Adrian VI. The college was originally housed in Adrian's residence, though it was systematically expanded with adjacent premises. The original complex was razed in 1775, and replaced with the present building.

The college of the Jesuits was located between the Pope's College and St. Michael's Church. In the history of science, it is primarily known for the famous mathematicians who taught there, like Gregorius a Sancto Vincento, Johannes Ciermans, and Andreas Tacquet. In 1773, the Jesuit order was dissolved. In the former Jesuit college, Empress Maria-Theresia founded the Collegium Veteranorum (Veterans' College) in 1778, where graduates in the priesthood could stay while waiting for an appointment in a parish. The long façade on the Sint-Michielstraat still bears witness to the college's former presence there.

Among Emperor Joseph II's most sweeping, controversial acts were his reforms in the training of priests, by founding a General Seminary in 1786. The new institution was located in the Pope's College. In order to accommodate the anticipated large number of students, the college was fully rebuilt and combined with the Veterans' College as well as two neighboring premises, the Van Winckele and De Bay colleges (on the Tiensestraat, across from the De Valk College). In 1789, however, the General Seminary had already been eliminated.

Under this French revolutionary regime, the Pope's College was a branch of Paris's Hôtel des Invalides, used in caring for injured or maimed former military. The military commander moved into the Veterans' College. On July 30, 1803, even Napoleon stopped by Leuven for a little while. He visited the Pope's College and the De Valk residential college, where the military hospital was headquartered.

At the opening of the State University (*Rijksuniversiteit*) in 1817, the town of Leuven reallocated the college buildings on the Hogeschoolplein. The Faculty of Letters and Philosophy was located in the Pope's College, the Faculty of Mathematics and Physics in the Veterans' College. In the latter college, the laboratory for chemistry was also set up.

In 1825, King William I (of the United Kingdom of the Netherlands) founded a Collegium Philosophicum (i.e., Filosofisch College, or Philosophical College), an official state seminary for training priests. The college was housed in the Pope's College and expanded into the Veterans' College. For purposes of the Philosophical College, two auditoriums were built (the Large and the Small Aula assembly halls) in the inner courtyard of the Veterans' College. One novelty was the installation of a steam heating system for these auditoriums, one of the first on the European continent.

At the inauguration of the Catholic University, the college buildings were again allotted by the town of Leuven free of charge. In 1837, the name of the Veterans' College was changed to the Maria-Theresia College, in reference to the empress who had established the Veterans' College.

The growing importance of laboratory instruction, which was felt from the 1860s forward, obliged the Faculty to convert more and more classrooms in the colleges into laboratories. The chemistry lab for Louis Henry was housed in the Pope's College; from 1882 to 1889, Jean-Baptiste Carnoy's lab for cell biology, too, until it was transferred to Villers College in the Vaartstraat. In the Maria-Theresia College, there were labs for general chemistry, analytical chemistry, and industrial chemistry for the newly established program in engineering that was located there from 1864 forward. These laboratories remained within the college until 1909, when the Institute for Chemistry (the Arenberg Institute, now the STUK Arts Center) opened in the Naamsestraat. After World War I, the engineering program gradually moved to the newly established institutes in the Arenberg Park campus in suburban Heverlee.

IN THE LABORATORY OF JEAN-BAPTISTE CARNOY

The figurehead for the laboratory movement at Leuven was Jean-Baptiste Carnoy. After being ordained as a priest, Carnoy did his training in the natural sciences at Leuven. Afterward he spent time at various German universities. In 1876, he was brought back to Leuven again to teach a practical course on microscopy. A few years later, he was also tasked with teaching botany, physiology of plants, plant paleontology, and plant diseases. His own scientific specialty was cytology. In addition, he was named inspector of the university's physical equipment and scientific collections.

Carnoy was of the opinion that you had to be able to observe and handle things yourself in order to understand them. Taking up his professorial duties, he resolved never to teach a class outside the laboratory. To do so, he had to provide the necessary resources himself. He bought (and paid with his own money!) some fifty microscopes and took care of the necessary examination tables and storage cabinets. From 1882 forward, he was able to make use of his own laboratory in the Pope's College. It consisted of three classrooms connected with one another. The largest classroom also served as an auditorium. There were 24 large tables, each with two or three microscopes. A small adjacent space was Carnoy's and his doctoral students' own research lab. The third classroom also served as a storage space for instruments, preparations, and lab animals in glass tanks.

One description from 1885 mentions no fewer than seventy microscopes, all of them produced by Carl Zeiss ,the renowned German manufacturer of optical devices, following instructions by Carnoy himself. Carnoy had met Zeiss in Jena while studying abroad in Germany. Carnoy also designed an original device for microphotography, which he had Zeiss build. It seems he never worked on it himself, however.

Jean Baptiste Carnoy.

At the start of each class, the students got assignments that they had to carry out in groups of two. His assistant and future colleague Gustave Gilson sketched how things happened in the lab. “That’s where you saw the master at work. He engaged every student, walking from one table to the next, helping them with his vast scientific knowledge and his astute observations. He taught the one group how to set up a rationale, the other how to rein in their all too unrestrained imaginations. He brought vitality, dedication, and enthusiasm. He was personally interested in each student. He became their friend, their confidant, their counselor. That created the great respect, the deep affection, the boundless devotion, which everyone attests to in having had the good fortune of being able to work with him.”[20]

With Carnoy, the students not only learned the practical fundamentals of microscopic examination. Carnoy also engaged the best students in his own research. That involvement concerned cellular division in the context of reproduction, a very sensitive topic in the late nineteenth century, given that the continuity of living cells transpired by way of lifeless particles of matter. So as to make his results (and those of his students) more easily known, he founded – as happened more often in specialized laboratories – his own journal: *La Cellule* (The Cell). Carnoy did not publish much on his own. On his students he impressed the golden rule: "If you want to publish, you must (1) have something to say; (2) say it; and (3) stop, as soon as you've said it."[21] Whoever reads the sometimes wide-ranging contributions in *La Cellule* may wonder whether Carnoy in fact applied his own rules with the requisite rigor.

Carnoy's laboratory enjoyed great success. Cytology was one of the new disciplines in biology (along with physiology and bacteriology) and the stage for major as well as rapid progress. Carnoy knew how to attract the best students. Many of them would develop careers of their own in the sciences, whether or not at Leuven. Upon his premature passing in 1899, his students carried on with his laboratory work. Just like Carnoy, notably, these successors were priests. Victor Grégoire continued Carnoy's research on the mechanism of cell division. Philibert Biourge worked on plant diseases and microbiology, and Alfons Janssens gained renown with his discovery of crossing-over in genetics.

The success of the Carnoy Institute (as Villers College was renamed in 1901) remained great. Even after World War I, the Institute's labs enjoyed their heydays. It saw a colorful mix of characters pass through: in Grégoire's laboratory, one student observed the presence of "Buddhists from Japan and priests from Flanders and Wallonia, medical students and Portuguese or Italian Franciscans, Polish professors and Spanish Jesuits, smart American girls and pious nuns."[22]

Carnoy's laboratory was a source of pride for the Catholic University. In official speeches, the lab was regularly presented as proof that the university had secured its place in the scientific world. And yet, the true flourishing of Leuven's laboratory research would not set in until after World War I, with the construction of a large number of new laboratories and access to better financing.

STOP NO. 5

KING'S COLLEGE

→ Naamsestraat 59

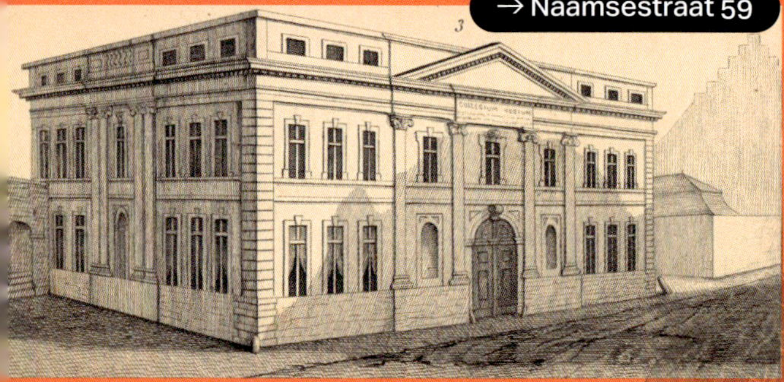

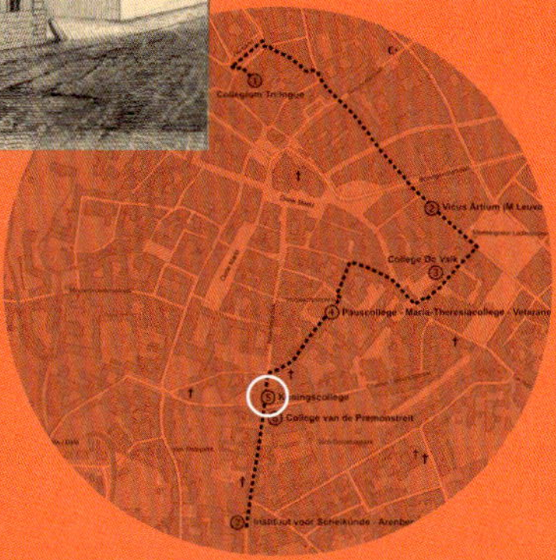

LIVING IN THE LABORATORY

The establishment of the State University saw to it that the colleges allocated by the town of Leuven would serve to accommodate not only the necessary collections and laboratories, but also housing for the professor in charge. The chemist Jean-Baptiste Van Mons lived in the Maria-Theresia College; the physicist Jean Ferdinand Sentelet in the Premonstratensian College; and Franz Joseph Adelmann, the professor for natural history, in the King's College.

Very little is known about the domestic life of the professors. Van Mons was a widower, and only two of his four sons (Charles and Théodore) supposedly lived with him in Leuven. Both of them finished their studies during the 1822–1823 academic year, as a physician and jurist, respectively. Van Mons continued to live in the college until he became emeritus in 1836, when he moved to a residence in the Tiensestraat.

Sentelet was already sixty years old when he was appointed professor at Leuven. He had studied theology at the Old University, but he clearly had gotten involved with the reform policies of the Austrian Habsburg authorities. Sentelet was probably unmarried. He retired after just a few years and died at his brother's in Overwinden, although his legal residence was still in Leuven. His successor at Leuven, however, did not live in the Premonstratensian College but in the Kattenstraat (the Charles De Bériotstraat) – unless this designation was for a side entrance to the college.

Adelmann, a German, married Marie Barbe Harbaur, ten years his senior and the sister of Leuven's rector, in 1818. The Adelmann and Harbaur families had already known each other longer than that. A year later, their son Leofried was born. In 1825, Adelmann's fourteen-year-old nephew Georg came to Leuven and lived with his uncle in the King's College. Georg studied at the Faculty of Mathematics and Physics, leaving for

The King's College around 1860.

Würzburg to continue his medical studies there in 1828. Later on, Georg would recall his uncle's German-speaking colleagues, in particular, as well as the foreign scholars who came to visit.

The custom of professors also residing in the college that housed their collection or laboratory was continued when the Catholic University was founded. Jacques-Guillaume Crahay, a former student of Minckelers in Maastricht, lived in the Premonstratensian College. That was also the case after Crahay with the physics professors Adrien Docq and Auguste Devivier. Another former student of Minckelers, Martin Martens, was named professor of chemistry and botany. He moved in to the King's College, however, and not into the Maria-Theresia College, which in its role as a residential college for students might not have offered much peace and quiet. In 1851, he moved to the Wezenstraat (Vital De Costerstraat), and his position in the King's College was taken by Pierre-Joseph Van Beneden.

Zoological collection in the King's College around 1900.

In the nineteenth century, it was not uncommon for professors to live in close proximity to their collections or laboratories. Before the major laboratory revolution during the 1870s, scientists often set up a private lab at home, where they would also train a few outstanding students. Even when the laboratories were built by a university, it was in its interest to provide the professor with accommodations in the building. Safety concerns were probably an important reason. A professor was able to keep an eye out in case of fire, or if something went wrong in the lab. Additionally, the proximity of the lab facilitated the professor's productivity, which was not tied to opening and closing times. An further argument was the importance of prestige. In Germany, especially, huge, monumental laboratories were built which included a spacious, luxurious residence for the professor.

At Leuven, that kind of majestic laboratory building was not affordable. The only exception was the Institute for Bacteriology. When it opened in 1899, it was praised as "un petit palais" (a little palace). It was also the residence (with a separate entrance) for Professor Joseph Denys, who lived there with his family. The 'pomp and circumstance' of the new building was made possible by the (promise of) income from the commercial production of vaccines. The way that income was spent, however, would later lead to major tensions between Denys and Leuven's rector.

And yet, for professors to live in their institutes had a few disadvantages as well. There was the inevitable tension between their private dwelling and the public space. Professor Van Mons's chemical lab was in reality just a small part of his kitchen, as someone demeaningly noted in 1833. The fact that Van Mons's successor moved into the King's College can perhaps be seen as an 'escape' from the restless atmosphere at Maria-Theresia College. Another disadvantage was that when the professor died, the entire family had to make way for their successor. Comfort levels in the old laboratory buildings were also questionable.

We know very little about the living conditions for professors in the colleges. Professor Crahay supposedly had two children, one of whom was a daughter, Laura, born in Leuven. It may be that Professor Devivier's parents lived with him. Little is said about family members in professors' obituaries. Pierre-Joseph Van Beneden, the oft-honored professor of comparative anatomy, is the only exception. When he first moved into the King's College, his family consisted of five persons: he himself, his spouse Rosalie Valcke, and their three children Augusta, Edouard, and Hélène. Three more girls were born in the King's College: Ernestine, Anne-Louise, and Marie-Thérèse. When he died, his widow and their two unmarried daughters moved to a house in the Statiestraat (Bondgenotenlaan).

How the Van Benedens and their many children lived in the King's College, which rooms were available to them, and how much space had to be reserved for the natural history collections is not known. Contemporaries praised Van Beneden for his tireless efforts to expand his natural history collection. From a small compilation, it had expanded into a full-fledged museum. His collection of whale skeletons was especially renowned. Once a year, it was opened to the public. In the college, in addition, he also had a private laboratory where he made and examined anatomical specimens. Sometimes neighbors would complain about the unbearable odor whenever Van Beneden brought a rotting whale carcass back to Leuven.

In 1868, Van Beneden addressed a request to the municipal administration – still responsible for structurally maintaining the colleges – to erect a small annex to put the skeleton of a very rare whale. Begrudgingly, the liberal burgomaster Henri Peemans agreed. "If Mr. Van Beneden finds the room in the natural history museum too small, then he can just go stay somewhere else,"[23] he remarked. The burgomaster also subtly noted that Van Beneden was living in the King's College at the town's expense, and he added that his remark also applied to the professor of physics in the Premonstratensian College.

Pierre-Joseph Van Beneden lived happily and undisturbed among his collections and laboratory. No doubt it was a peculiar experience for Van Beneden's family and must

P.-J. VAN BENEDEN (1809-1894)

Pierre-Joseph Van Beneden. Lithograph by Jean Malvaux (1907).

have made a deep impression. His son Edouard followed in the footsteps of his father. He became a professor in Liège, where he had a splendid new laboratory building, including a professor's residence, built. His older sister Auguste married Professor Constant Vanlair, who would set up labs for microscopy and physiology in Liège.

At the beginning of the twentieth century, the model for the resident professor was seemingly outdated. Just about all professors in the Faculty of Sciences were living in private residences, some of them even outside the town. Only in the Carnoy Institute were there three professors still, all of them clergy. The King's College provided a place for Professor Gustave Gilson, though he actually lived in Herent. A few colleges, though, did still provide space for a concierge to live.

One exception is the residence of Henry de Dorlodot, a priest and theologian. He was brought by Cardinal Mercier to Leuven in 1889, to teach at the newly established Institute of Philosophy, though disagreements about the doctrine to be followed led to conflict. De Dorlodot was appointed at the Faculty of Sciences in the paleontology curriculum for mining engineers, later supplemented with the program in geology. With his own resources, De Dorlodot put together a geological and paleontological collection, which he located in his own brand new private home at Charles de Bériotstraat 32-34. Built in 1897, his home was expanded in 1905 with a second building, the Coal Museum (Kolenmuseum). De Dorlodot – who, in addition to his conflict with Mercier, was also a major proponent of Darwinism – remained something of an outsider at Leuven. Having his own museum offered him a certain degree of independence. After his death, the complex remained property of his heirs; it was not until 1948 that it was transferred to the university.

STOP NO. 5 – KING'S COLLEGE

The King's College was founded by King Philip II (the son of Emperor Charles) in 1579, for the purpose of housing and training theology students preparing to work as priests in the Northern Netherlands. In its first years, the college was located in the empty buildings of the College of the Holy Spirit. In 1589, it moved to its present location, where an existing "thuys van Ath" (Ath residence) was purchased. Little is known about this original college building.

In 1775, Jan-Frans Thysbaert – the president of the King's College, in addition to being a professor of philosophy and director of the School for Experimental Physics – received permission (and the means) to renovate the college. Little remained of the original structure. The new building was erected in neoclassical style, possibly following the plans of the Leuven architect Martinus Ghenne, who was also responsible, among other things, for the renovation of the Pope's College. It might also be possible, though, to attribute the building to the architect connected to the Austrian Habsburg court, Laurent-Benoît Dewez, who had previously already worked on the Vicus Artium.

When the State University was installed in 1817, the natural history collections were housed in the King's College. It continued in this capacity during the transition to the Catholic University in 1835. In the nineteenth century, the collections were substantially expanded by Professor Pierre-Joseph Van Beneden. In the process, emphasis was placed on zoology, paleontology, and comparative anatomy. For more than two hundred years the college was used as a location for the program in Zoology.

Over the years, the college was rebuilt several times. The biggest modifications took place in 1938. At that time, the eastern wing of the college was razed and replaced with a U-shaped addition on the site of the college's former garden. In May 1944, the college was hit hard by the Allied bombing of Leuven. A large part of the collection was lost in the process. Even so, the current Museum for Zoology in the college's museum hall constitutes a varied, instructive ensemble.

THE LAURELS OF PIERRE-JOSEPH VAN BENEDEN

Pierre-Joseph Van Beneden died on January 8, 1894, a few weeks after his eighty-fourth birthday. Until the very end, he remained active as a researcher and teacher. His career as a professor lasted no less than 58 years. In his eulogy, Rector Abbeloos expressed what Van Beneden had meant to the university: "*Cecidit corona capitis nostri*. The crown has fallen from our head."[24] He made an enormous impression on the students as well. "They came to class with complete respect for this highly educated man, though soon enough – without any weakening whatsoever of that respect – they felt that distance between master and student diminish. His appearance was so friendly, his speech so gentle – he was so humble, in other words – that he was able to put his knowledge within their youthful grasp. [...] Yes, it was a genuine treat for us every time we could go listen to Van Beneden."[25]

Van Beneden was not just a gifted speaker. He was also the most celebrated of Leuven's professors. In the university's *Annuaire* – the annual publication that presented the professors and announced the course schedule – the list of scholarly distinctions and memberships in academic societies under Van Beneden's name took up an entire page.

Van Beneden received his greatest accolade in January 1854. Two years earlier, the Parisian Academy had held a competition regarding the development of intestinal parasites and their transmission from one animal to the next. Holding such competitions was a very common practice in the nineteenth century, primarily with the goal of settling a current debate. Very little was yet known about intestinal parasites. Scientists did not even agree about the classification of the different species, even less so about their origination and reproduction. Some scholars believed in a kind of spontaneous generation, while others thought that the parasites could, anatomically speaking, pretty much limitlessly adapt themselves to the environment they were in.

Van Beneden sent in a treatise about tapeworms. He showed how the life cycle of tapeworms played out in the various animals that served as 'hosts.' His study rejected the idea of any spontaneous generation and proved that these organisms, which until then had been considered to be different parasites, were in reality different developmental phases of the same parasite. Van Beneden was able to follow the development of intestinal parasites by the hour. He had made his discovery already in 1850, by examining fish in his private laboratory in Oostende, yet expanded his experiments in Leuven to dogs and rabbits.

Van Beneden went to Paris to receive his prize of 6,000 francs in person. Returning to Leuven , he was given a celebratory reception. More than 400 students marched in a parade from University Hall to the train station where they, along with numerous residents from town, festively greeted Professor Van Beneden. In a horse-drawn carriage, Van Beneden was taken to Rector De Ram, where the entire academic administration was waiting for him. In the evening, a torchlit procession went through the streets and a serenade in honor of the laureate was performed for an audience. During an open session of the town council a few days later, Van Beneden received a gold medal in the Gothic Hall of the town hall. The city of Mechelen, Van Beneden's birthplace, also came to Leuven with a delegation to congratulate the professor.

In 1862, Van Beneden was the guest of honor once again in the Gothic Hall. This time, the municipal administration bestowed upon him a medal of honor because he had just been awarded the Five-Year State Prize for Natural Sciences. In the end, Van Beneden won this prize three times.

Medal of honor for Pierre-Joseph Van Beneden for his fiftieth anniversary as professor (1886).

On the occasion of his fourtieth anniversary as professor, his students gave him a marble bust created by the Belgian sculptor Charles Fraikin. From the city of Mechelen, too, he received another medal of honor.

Even grander was the ceremony in honor of the fiftieth anniversary of his appointment as professor. On June 20, 1886, a large crowd gathered in the auditorium of the Pope's College, including Minister of Education Joseph Thonissen, Rector Constant Pieraerts, Burgomaster of Leuven Leopold Vanderkelen, numerous professors, politicians, and domestic and foreign scholars. During the academic convocation, Van Beneden was given gold, silver, and bronze copies of a medal of honor. He received a bronze statue from his past and present students: *L'Étude et la Méditation* (Study and Meditation) by the French artist Paul Dubois.

On this occasion, too, Van Beneden was showered with honors. He was named grand officer in the Order of Leopold as well as officer in the French *Légion d'Honneur*. The city of Mechelen gave him another medal of honor with his likeness and announced that one of the city ramparts would be renamed the Van Benedenlaan. A bust was placed on Mechelen's city hall. Rector Pieraerts had another, special homage: he declared that Van Beneden would *not* be given emeritus status, but that he could remain a professor "as long as he shall live."

Even after his death, the honors did not stop. Scant days after his passing, the town council decided to rename the rather modest Eierenstraat as Pierre-Joseph Van Beneden-straat. His funeral in St. Michael's Church was attended by many students, colleagues, and professors from other universities. From then on, the King's College was designated the Van Beneden Institute. In 1897, a biography by the Antwerp hydrologist Adolphe Kemna appeared. One year later, the city of Mechelen put a life-size statue of Van Beneden in place. It bore the inscription: "To the world-famous natural historian and professor."

STOP NO. 6

PREMONSTRATENSIAN COLLEGE

→ Naamsestraat 61

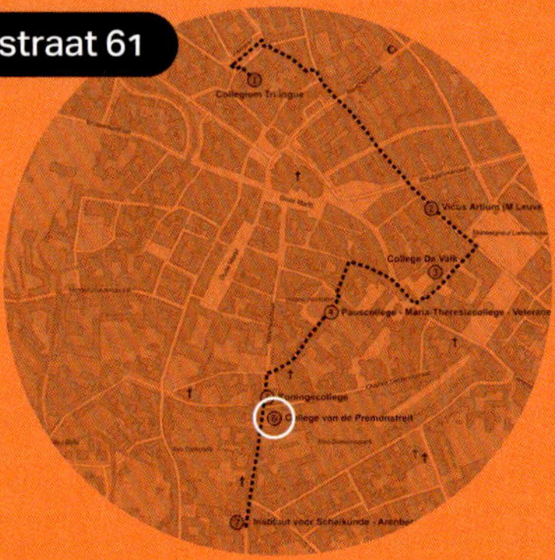

ON THE INTERNATIONAL STAGE

For some time, the Catholic University had trouble proving itself to be a scientific institution. During the nineteenth century, it was attacked more than once, under the assumption that on account of its religious convictions, it would not be able to answer to the demands of science for independent and objective research. Jan Stas, an alumnus of the State University at Leuven, called the university an "anachronism in the intellectual world."[26] Catholics were feeling cornered, or as a Catholic journalist ironically observed, "It's well known that Catholics are the worst enemies of all progressive scientific systems."[27]

Naturally, the Catholic University saw things differently. In its view, it was the Catholic faith, in fact, that provided something to hold onto in a rapidly developing world. Without faith, modern science led only to doubt and dismay. This vision was embodied by the biologist Pierre-Joseph Van Beneden, for whom investigating nature brought humanity first and foremost into contact with Creation. The general esteem for Van Beneden's work had positive effects for the university. Yet behind the many tributes paid, a relative level of scarcity was hiding: except for Van Beneden, the university had produced few big names that meant anything in the scientific world.

Introducing the German laboratory model changed that situation. Universities were presumed to carry out original research as well as educate students in it. That required well-outfitted laboratories with advanced equipment and a responsive expansion of the workforce. For the Catholic University at Leuven, which largely depended on donations from wealthy Catholic burghers, these needs were not easy to achieve. When, in 1881, Rector Pieraerts proudly announced that the Catholic University could compete with the best institutions abroad, the Faculty of Sciences reacted vehemently. Leuven's labs did not meet international standards

The Premonstratensian College, known as the Institute for Physics from 1817 forward.

at all. The university had to get to work urgently on creating new laboratories because – the Faculty contended – especially a Catholic university could not afford to lag behind in scientific advances.

Yet the university could only meet the demand for researchers with some difficulty. New research labs were as yet still beyond the financial capacities of the university. Among other things, the mounting costs for the engineering program and the recently established Agriculture School left little room for structural investment. In 1882, after stepping down as rector, Monsignor Namèche donated his private home in the Minderbroedersstraat, where three laboratories were immediately located for the Faculty of Medicine. In the same street, a few more buildings were bought for the Agriculture School, and labs were set up here as well. In 1888, Carnoy was able to move his laboratories in the Pope's College to Villers College. Modifications and renovations were always involved. The first new laboratories did not come about until the rectorship of Adolphe Hebbelynck and then the Institute for Bacteriology (1899), the Institute for Electromechanics in the Vlamingenstraat (1900), the Institute for Medical Pathology in the Minderbroedersstraat (1906), and the Institute for Chemistry in the Naamsestraat (1909).

The natural sciences gained – certainly as far as investments were concerned – more and more importance (in that respect, we can also take into account the relatively new disciplines within medicine, like experimental physiology and bacteriology). And what about the label "Catholic"? Most of the professors stayed on the sidelines and left major pronouncements to their theologically trained colleagues. Professor Désiré Mercier, the future archbishop, established the Institute of Philosophy in 1889, with the explicit mission of providing the modern natural sciences with a philosophical framework, inspired by the scholastic thought of the thirteenth-century theologian Thomas Aquinas. Among other things, the curriculum comprised courses in the natural sciences, for which professors from the Faculty of Sciences were engaged. Labs for physics and chemistry were even set

The physics laboratory in the Premonstratensian College ca. 1900.

up in the Institute, which elicited from Rector Abbeloos – who was not favorably inclined toward Mercier's program – the scornful remark: "Il n'y a pas de chimie catholique, moins encore thomiste"[28] (There isn't any Catholic chemistry, much less one that is Thomist). Abbeloos had to give in and was replaced by the aforementioned Hebbelynck.

Until World War I, despite every effort, science at Leuven remained underrepresented on the national and international level. Between 1886 and 1918, only one professor at Leuven became a member of the Royal Academy for the Sciences. Only two professors received a State Prize during the same period.

How and why that situation changed after World War I can be explained through a number of factors. The most decisive was the increase in available funding. In 1922, the Belgian state decided to award the private universities (Leuven and Brussels) an annual operations subsidy, equal to sixty percent of what the state universities received. In addition, Leuven was able to make use of the resources from Herbert Hoover's Commission for Relief in Belgium. Donations came less from private benefactors than from industrial businesses. The Belgian American Educational Foundation (BAEF) made travel stipends to the United States available to promising researchers. Various professors had spent time during the war years at universities in the Netherlands, Great Britain, and France, which gave them a stronger international orientation. From 1928 forward, research projects could be financed through the National Fund for Scientific Research. As a result, a larger group of researchers and research assistants could be employed at any one laboratory.

This development was most remarkable in physics. Until World War I, physics was taught primarily as basic science, subordinate to more lucrative programs in chemistry, medicine, and industrial science. Revolutionary developments, though, like the discovery of X-rays – as well as the formulation of the theory of relativity and quantum mechanics – opened up new perspectives. Their impact was clearly noticeable in the Premonstratensian College. A striking example is the physicist Charles Manneback. He graduated as a mining engineer in 1920, and left for a year with a stipend from the BAEF for MIT in Cambridge, MA, where he received his doctorate. After his appointment at Leuven, he arranged his teaching in such a way that he had one semester free for travel. Manneback went to work with (future) Nobel Prize recipients Peter Debye in Zürich, Werner Heisenberg in Leipzig, Niels Bohr in Copenhagen, and Enrico Fermi in Rome.

Another example was Georges Lemaître, who was ordained as a priest after his studies at Leuven, having in the meantime devoted himself to the theory of relativity. After his ordination as priest, he left for a year at the University of Cambridge and afterward another at Harvard and MIT. In 1927, he published his theory of the expanding universe in a rather obscure Catholic science journal. It was barely noticed. In 1931, however, he published his revolutionary theory of the Big Bang in the authoritative journal *Nature*. The theory garnered much criticism, though it gained support from Einstein. Lemaître met Einstein four times, twice in Brussels, once in California, and once at Princeton.

International influence was also noticeable when instruction in the sciences underwent 'Dutchification' (*vernederlandsing*). In physics, Augustin Van Itterbeek was hired. Van Itterbeek had studied at Ghent and Leiden, concentrating his investigative work on the study of gases and liquids at low temperatures. After four years of research, he succeeded in making helium fluid by means of a liquefactor he had developed – something that until then had only succeeded at Leiden, Moscow, Oxford, and Cambridge. Van Itterbeek, too, published his results in *Nature*, as by that point international publications had become the norm.

The ambitions of Leuven's physicists reached even higher. Marc de Hemptinne studied the properties of radioisotopes, yet understood that the cyclotron – a new kind of device developed at Berkeley – was most appropriate for that purpose. In 1938, he himself left for Berkeley to negotiate the purchase of a cyclotron with Ernest Lawrence. He sent two of his associates to Berkeley and additionally consulted with the team of Frédéric Joliot-Curie in Paris, where they were also working on building a cyclotron. As a result of the war, it would take until 1952, before Leuven would be able to have a cyclotron. The cyclotron would not be placed in the Premonstratensian College, however, but in a new institute in suburban Heverlee.

STOP NO. 6 – PREMONSTRATENSIAN COLLEGE

The designation Premonstratensian refers to the Premonstratensian Order, founded in the twelfth century by Norbert of Xanten in Prémontré, in northern France. Members of the order were also called Norbertines or White Canons. In the Southern Netherlands in 1571, the Norbertine abbeys of Park, Averbode, Grimbergen, and Ninove founded the Premonstratensian College in de Naamsestraat for the education of their own theology professors. Later, most of the other Norbertine abbeys joined them.

In the middle of the eighteenth century, the old college was razed and replaced by a building in the style of Louis XV. In the original plans, the ground floor of the college was elevated. From the courtyard, you reached the entrance by way of an impressive staircase with a flight of stairs on either side. Behind the college wing, there were expansive vegetable and pleasure gardens.

When the university was abolished in 1797, the building was used as the court of first instance (or trial court). From 1810 onward, it served as a military hospital. When the State University was established, the collections for physics and also, initially, for mineralogy were located there.

The building was modified on a regular basis. In 1890, the staircase disappeared; in 1903, the original entrance gate was partially razed. The original cartouches with the building's inscription "COLLEGIUM CANONICORUM PRAEMONSTRATENSIUM 1755" can still be viewed in the courtyard.

In the 1930s, a second wing was built behind the college building, intended for classrooms and laboratories. It was also where the large collection of physics instruments was housed. During Allied bombings in the night from May 11 to 12, 1944, this rear building was reduced to ashes. More than ninety percent of the instruments collection was lost.

In 1972, a new physics building was launched in Heverlee. Since then, the Premonstratensian College has been used primarily for teaching, serving as such for the Faculty of Economics and Business since 2015.

GEORGES LEMAÎTRE ON FAITH AND SCIENCE

In 2017, KU Leuven unveiled a bust of Georges Lemaître in the courtyard of the Premonstratensian College. The unveiling was part of a two-day homage, one day in Leuven and one day Louvain-la-Neuve. It is somewhat ironic that Lemaître – the first to show that the space all around us keeps getting bigger, and that all objects in space are being driven further away from one another – has now become a symbol of the renewed rapprochement between the two sister schools, a good half century after the Catholic University was split in two.

For many years, Lemaître had his office at the Premonstratensian College. He was named an instructor there in 1925; Lemaître was already 34 years old at the time. He had come to Leuven in 1911, to take courses to become a mining engineer. When World War I broke out, he volunteered for army

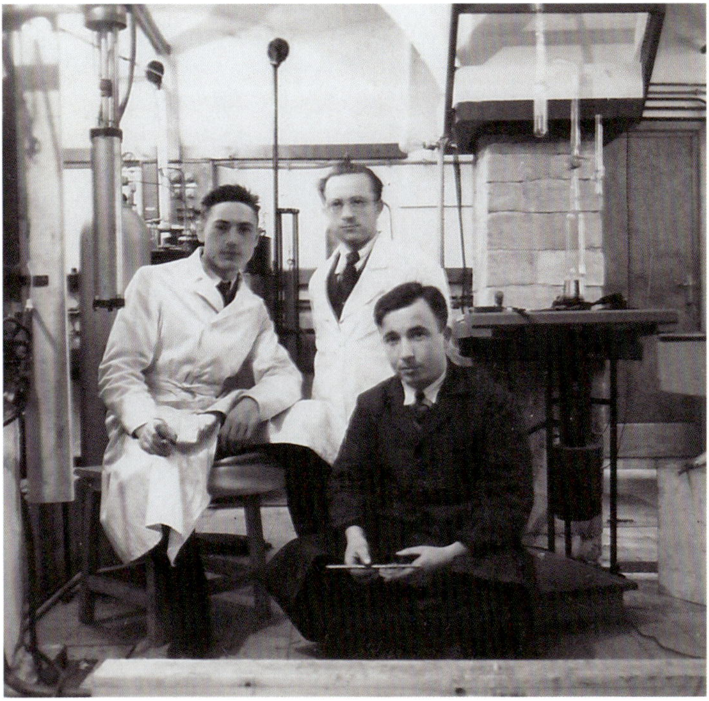

Research assistants in the laboratory of Prof. Augustin Van Itterbeek (1937).

service. After the war, he continued his studies at Leuven, yet concentrated now on physics. After he graduated, he enrolled in the Seminary at Mechelen (for those called late to the priesthood) and was ordained as a priest on September 22, 1923. In the years that followed, he travelled to England, Canada, and the United States. He obtained his PhD at MIT in Cambridge, MA, and was promoted to professor at Leuven in 1927.

From the very start, it was clear that the university had high hopes with Lemaître's appointment. The theory of relativity, developed by Albert Einstein in 1905, had not drawn the attention of physicists in Belgium until relatively late. From the 1920s forward, though, along with the just as revolutionary quantum mechanics, this theory was presented as a beacon for modern science. In it liberals saw the harbinger of a major turnaround in ideologies that had rusted shut.

STOP NO. 6

Catholics, however, saw in these new theories an indication of the crisis that Western science had come to.

At Leuven, Lemaître taught courses about the theory of relativity, mathematical astronomy, methodology of physics, and history of science. Yet it was not so much with his teaching – not everyone was that thrilled with his didactic qualities – but with his research that Lemaître proved to be a leading authority in physics, one who made up part of a small, select group of physicists at the foundation of one of the greatest scientific revolutions in history.

In 1927, Lemaître presented a model of the cosmos in which space was not static but constantly expanding. With this model, it was possible to explain why all astronomical objects appear to be distancing themselves from one another. And Lemaître went further: if the universe is becoming larger and larger, it must have been quite a lot smaller in the past. Lemaître took this notion all the way back to *l'atome primitif*, the primeval atom in which the entire universe had once been concentrated. The theory was mocked later on as the 'Big Bang' theory, a phrase that has since become commonplace. Lemaître looked his entire life for concrete proof of the theory, which according to him, had to be found in cosmic radiation. That intuition turned out to be correct. The so-called background radiation from the Big Bang was indeed observed in cosmic radiation by two American physicists (Arno Penzias and Robert Wilson) in 1964, earning them both the Nobel Prize in 1978. For Lemaître, though, the recognition came too late: he died in 1966.

The theory of the Big Bang had far-reaching consequences. The world as we know it did and will not last forever. Once there was a starting point from which arose everything that we now observe. The fact that this theory was developed by a Catholic priest raised more than a few questions. According to the Catholic faith, the world is created by God. The hypothesis that the universe had a starting point comes very close to this

Bust of Georges Lemaître in the courtyard of the Premonstratensian College.

religious vision of the world and could be interpreted as a new form for the proof of God.

In any case, that view was the opinion of Pope Pius XII who, in an address to the Papal Academy in 1951, referred to the Big Bang theory as confirmation for the Creation in Scripture. Lemaître – himself a member of the Papal Academy – did not agree and made that clear to the pope. In the end, Pius XII changed the text of his address and wisely left out any interpretation of concrete scientific theories.

How Lemaître saw the relationship between science and faith is fodder for debate even today. Over the course of his life, his stance evolved. As a young priest, he was firmly convinced that science would ultimately confirm the truth of the Bible. Yet one of his professors at the Seminary in Mechelen talked him out of that idea. If the Bible already concurred with modern scientific insights, that was mere coincidence. It is wrong to think that the Bible must be read as a science textbook.

In his later years, Lemaître became more inclined toward a two-way model. Faith and science each spoke in their own way and within their own domains about truth. As long as we respect that distinction, there is no conflict between faith and science. "Science has not shaken my faith in religion, and religion has never caused me to question the conclusions I reached by strictly scientific methods,"[29] Lemaître said in an interview. Lemaître found the key to this two-way model not in any strict theological doctrine, but in a personal open-mindedness with regard to the mysteries of existence.

In any case, Lemaître did not want the scientific debate over his theories to be influenced by religious arguments. He therefore emphasized the fundamental distinction between 'beginning' and 'creation.' The Big Bang was the beginning of the world as we know it now. It is not possible for scientists to say anything about what happened before that moment in time. The observable beginning of the world, however, does not coincide with the origin of the world. Creation preceded the primeval atom. The hypothesis of the primeval atom, in fact, puts a limit to the human capacity for being able to say anything about the origin of the world by way of science. God remains hidden to science and is revealed only to the one who believes.

STOP NO. 7

INSTITUTE FOR CHEMISTRY (ARENBERG INSTITUTE)

→ Naamsestraat 69

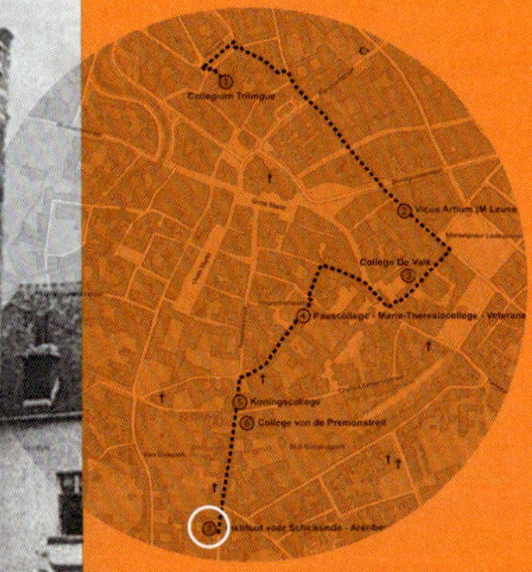

LABORATORIES IN THE PARK

An end to the university's close quarters in the colleges of the Old University finally came about under the rectorship of Adolphe Hebbelynck (1898–1909). For the Faculty of Sciences, the Institute for Electromechanics was built in the Vlamingenstraat (1900), the Institute for Zootechnics in the Minderbroedersstraat (1909), and the Institute for Chemistry in the Naamsestraat (1909). The largest construction projects, though, would not come until the following administration of Rector Paulin Ladeuze.

After taking office in 1909, Ladeuze laid out his vision for the university as a center of science. The university did not exist just to impart established knowledge, but also to generate new knowledge The acquisition of scientific knowledge was a goal in and of itself, only in second place was it to be focussed on practical applications. At Leuven, students could be infused with the intellectual life of academe, which would best prepare them for their future role in society.

To make that goal reality, Ladeuze started an impressive building campaign for adapting the university's material infrastructure to the needs of contemporary science. Attention was given first of all to the humanities. The Faculties for Theology and Law, as well as the School for Political and Social Sciences, were housed in the new Spoelberch Institute (Naamsestraat). The new building for the Business School – located on the corner of the Andreas Vesaliusstraat and the Dekenstraat – was still able to open before World War I broke out. The exact sciences were not forgotten, either. The Carnoy Institute (Villers College) was expanded with two wings for the installation of laboratories, while plans were made for transferring a number of labs to an ultramodern laboratory building in the Dekenstraat. The Institute for Physiology (since 1996: the CLT [Centrum voor Levende Talen] Language Centre)

Front elevation of the Arenberg Institute around 1930.

could be completed in 1915, and would grow into an important center for medical research after the war.

Reforms also found their way into the engineering program. Legislation from 1890 had officially recognized the program at Leuven, but the position of Leuven's engineers with respect to engineers educated at state universities was still problematic. Leuven was committed to a broad, scientific education but also needed to answer to the specializations of legally recognized degrees. At the initiative of the Engineers' Union from Leuven's

Design study (1961), indicating the areas for the Catholic University's expansion in Heverlee.

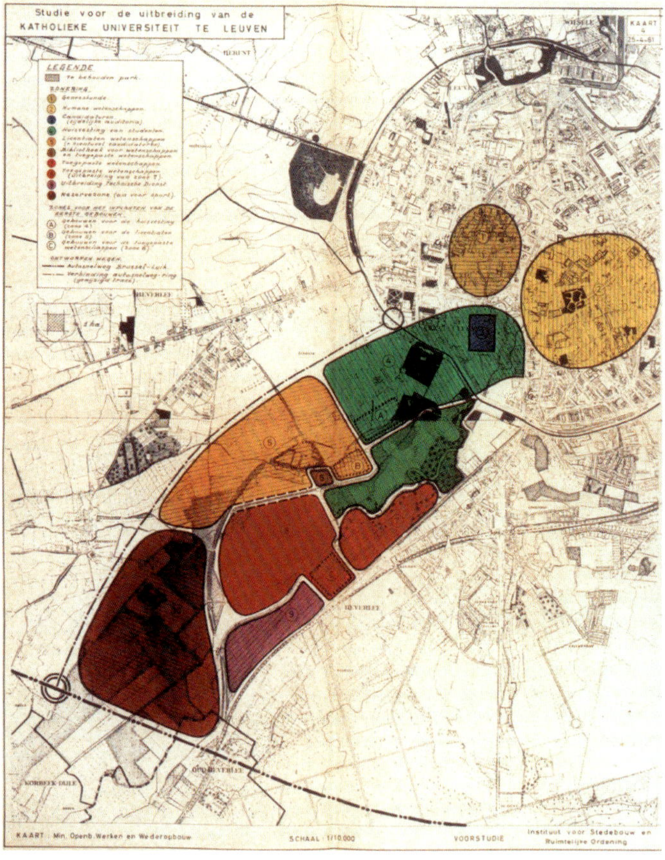

Special Schools (Unie der Ingenieurs uit de Leuvense Speciale Scholen, or UILv), work was carried out for sweeping curricular reforms. In that context, it was suggested for the first time that the laboratories and auditoriums needed could be built outside the town center on the old military training grounds at the Parkpoort (or Park Gate, now the location of the athletic complex "Sportoase" and of the former Philips buildings).

The plan did not go through, but right before World War I, the duke of Arenberg had let it be known that he wanted to donate his castle in Heverlee to the university. In doing so, he would also sell a portion of the surrounding park at a reasonable price. The university was prepared to enter into the deal, but the transaction could not take place on account of the war. Only in 1921 did the transfer become a fact. In the years that followed, a campus arose here based on the American model, planted at a distance from the town's core in the verdant landscape of Arenberg Park.

Although there were no building plans for the new institutes, the first stone was laid on November 11, 1922, at the fiftieth anniversary of the UILv. Only at the beginning of 1925 did the construction work start. An inaugural ceremony took place in 1928, but the work underwent major delays because, among other things, the university's other construction projects got priority. In order to finance the project, Count Eugène de Grunne set up a non-profit organization, the *Cité Universitaire d'Héverlé*, which collected the financial means primarily from the business community. Ultimately, the new buildings on the Willem de Croylaan could be launched in the 1931–32 academic year: the Institute for Industrial Chemistry and Metallurgy as well as the Thermotechnical Institute. In addition, Arenberg Castle itself needed to be customized for teaching topography, civil engineering, and architecture.

Five years later, the construction of the Agricultural Institute – according to plans made by Raymond Lemaire – was begun in the park. Financing came from the Ministry for Public Works in the framework of a national campaign to create job opportunities after the severe economic crisis of the early 1930s. Additionally, by way of alumni from the former

Agriculture School, a fundraising drive was set up, enlisting both individual donors and agricultural businesses and federations. In the summer of 1938, moving the laboratories out of the Minderbroedersstraat could begin. In June 1939, the new building was officially inaugurated.

With the construction of these institutes in Arenberg Park, moving the exact sciences out to suburban Heverlee had commenced. For the time being, however, the pure sciences remained in the town center. Both the Premonstratensian College (1934–35) and the King's College (1937–1939) were expanded with new rear wings in the years prior to World War II. There turned out to be little enthusiasm for moving to Heverlee. After World War II, when an appropriate location was sought for establishing a new Institute for Nuclear Physics, they first thought of embedding it where the Social Sciences Campus now is, close to the Institute for Pharmacy. On account of safety considerations, that plan did not go through. Even during the 1960s, when a move to Heverlee seemed inevitable, Professor Van Itterbeek fought tooth and nail against the forced relocation.

The scope of Ladeuze's building program between the two world wars does not become entirely clear until we consider – in addition to the sites already mentioned above – the reconstruction of the destroyed University Hall, the construction of the new University Library on the Volksplaats square (now Monsignor Ladeuzeplein), the Cancer Institute and various buildings of the Academic Hospital on the Kapucijnenvoer, and the Institute for Physical Education. On the Lovenjoel country estate donated by the de Spoelberch family, a new Zootechnical Institute was built – replacing the infrastructure on the Kapucijnenvoer – as well as a psychiatric institution for women. In Bierbeek, Ladeuze built the Sint-Kamillus University Psychiatric Center.

In this undertaking, Ladeuze was assisted by the buildings inspector, Canon Jan Janssen, who gradually acted more and more as builder and architect. In their history of the university at Leuven, Jan Roegiers and Emiel Lamberts judge the idiosyncratic yet dynamic developer with some reservations:

"Jansen had even less aesthetic sense than the rector, but he managed to develop a practical talent that was openly praised at his death by a man of the trade, Professor P. de Smet."[30] The building projects of Ladeuze and Jansen did not translate into daring, contemporary designs. Even where architects – like Emile Goethals, the Leuven professor of architecture – drew up the plans, the designs attest to a conservative style. In his classes, Goethals was opposed to the avant-garde ideas of a Le Corbusier. Canon Raymond Lemaire, who drafted the Agricultural Institute in Heverlee, also took inspiration from a Christian/historical aesthetic.

Under Rector Honoré Van Waeyenbergh, the great exodus of science laboratories from Leuven's town center would continue after World War II. Although his first task would involve restoring the university as quickly as possible from the damages suffered during the war, Van Waeyenbergh was also facing sharp growth in student numbers. He was also aware of continuing developments in scientific research and the need for modern laboratories. New institutes were built at a rapid pace, all of them in the Arenberg Science Park: the Electrotechnology Institute (1948), to replace the building in the Vlamingenstraat, which had suffered major damage during the war; and an Institute for Civil Engineering (1948), to expand the Institute for Industrial Chemistry and Metallurgy.

The new campus for the Faculty of Sciences on the Celestijnenlaan (1986).

Now for the first time, too, part of the natural science research was brought out to Heverlee. In 1949, the first phase in constructing the Institute for Atomic Research was completed. Construction had been made possible by a donation of ten million Belgian francs (roughly 250,000 euros) from the Union Minière du Haut-Katanga (Mining Union of Upper-Katanga, a Belgian mining company in today's Democratic Republic of the Congo). In the years that followed, a Van de Graaff particle accelerator and a cyclotron for the production of radioisotopes were installed in a separate annex. During the 1950s at Leuven, Professor Marc de Hemptinne was the central figure in nuclear research in Belgium. Plans were continually being made for further expansion. In 1962, it was decided to look for a more suitable location. In the end, the cyclotron research would relocate to Louvain-la-Neuve. The main building left behind was converted to the Institute of Botany and Microbiology.

In the 1960s, the university's geographical distribution across Leuven's center and Arenberg Park was officially taken up in university policy. In 1961, a commission drafted a plan to group the university's buildings around three poles. Inasmuch as possible, the humanities would remain in the town center. The exact sciences were grouped together in Heverlee, while the medical campus would be developed around the St. Peter and St. Raphaël clinics. Soon afterward, another option came up for this last campus: the Gasthuisberg district. After 1970, this land-use model of three clusters remained the core of the university's construction program.

The Arenburg Campus arose on the Celestijnenlaan between 1965 and 1972, with classrooms and laboratories for mathematics, physics, and chemistry. Buildings in the center of town were systematically vacated. The Institute for Earth (and Environmental) Sciences – located in the former Boys' Orphanage in the Redingenstraat since 1968 – moved to a brand new Geo-Institute in Heverlee in 2005. Today only the Institute for Zoology in the King's College and the adjacent Coal Museum are still in operation. Mid-2026, they too will move to the new BioScience Centre on Arenberg Campus. Then the last laboratory college in Leuven proper will have closed its doors.

STOP NO. 7 – INSTITUTE FOR CHEMISTRY (ARENBERG INSTITUTE)

On May 9, 1909, amid great interest, the brand new Institute for Chemistry was ceremoniously opened in the Naamsestraat. The building had come about through a magnanimous donation from the Arenberg family. In the original agreement, the duke of Arenberg pledged to absorb all the building's costs on his behalf: its maintenance, insurance, and all other expenses. The building remained the property of the Arenberg family but was made available free of charge "aussi longtemps que l'Université de Louvain [...] serait maintenue comme Université catholique" [31] (for as long as the University of Leuven [...] will be maintained as a Catholic University).

The architect for the building was Victor Lenertz, an instructor from Luxembourg in Leuven's engineering program, himself a student and assistant of Joris Helleputte. Just like Helleputte, Lenertz found inspiration in the neo-Gothic style, though he also had an eye for functionality and contemporary design. In 1900, Lenertz had also designed the Institute for Electromechanics in the Vlamingenstraat (now the Vlerick Business School).

When the new Institute opened, the labs had not yet been installed. Sculptures by Constant Meunier were put up in the empty halls. From 1887 to 1895, Meunier had worked as a painting teacher at Leuven's Art Academy, moving into a studio in the old Anatomical Theater in the Minderbroedersstraat.

The Arenberg Institute was taken over by the various chemistry and industrial chemistry labs, which until then had been housed in the Maria-Theresia College. At the opening, the centuries-old collaboration between the university and the Arenberg family was pointed out, in particular the research that Minckelers and Thysbaert had carried out at the duke's request. Commemoratively, two bas-reliefs with images of Minckelers and the duke were placed on the interior wall next to the entry.

Just three years after its opening, the building already proved to be too small. There was talk of an extra wing for installing three new laboratories for, respectively, pharmaceutical chemistry, Galenic pharmacy, and microscopy. As a result of the war, though, these projects could not be immediately carried out.

On July 28, 1924, a fire in the laboratory for industrial chemistry again pointed out the need for expansion. One professor saw the hand of God in the fire: "Puisse cet incendie faire hâter la réalisation des nouveaux laboratoires. C'est peut-être ce que le Bon Dieu a voulu!" [32] (May this fire hasten the creation of new laboratories. Perhaps it is what the Good Lord wanted!) Yet even the limited expansion between the wars was not enough for long. In 1956, the Arenberg Institute expanded again with two impressive wings around a rectangular inner courtyard, located on the Schapenstraat (now the Holleberg residence), based on a design by the architecture professor Emile Goethals.

The Arenberg Institute remained in use until the 1970s, when most of the labs moved to the new Institute for Chemistry on the Campus Celestijnenlaan 200 in suburban Heverlee. Starting in 1981, the building served as the location for dance performances or art exhibitions held by Leuven's student organization for culture, "Stuc." In 2000, the university (still owner of the building) concluded a lease agreement with Stuc (which transformed into STUK, beginning in 2001). The building was renovated by Neutelings Riedijk Architects, who later on were also responsible for the construction of Antwerp's Museum aan de Stroom (a.k.a. The MAS).

From November 2021 to June 2023, STUK was closed again for a thorough renovation, once more under the direction of Neutelings Riedijk Architects. During this renovation, the building was made more energy efficient, and modifications were implemented that are to promote the accessibility and openness of this home for culture.

WALTER MUND AND BELGIAN RADIUM

In 1896, French physicist Henri Becquerel discovered that uranium ore would spontaneously radiate and leave traces on a photographic plate. He called the phenomenon radioactivity. Not much later, Marie Curie succeeded in identifying a few of the most radioactive elements. Radium, in particular, proved to be powerfully radioactive. From 1900 forward, radium was used as a source of radiation in treating skin cancer.

Radium therapy offered a number of advantages compared to similar treatments with X-rays. From radium the low level radioactive and short-lived radon could be derived, a noble gas that could relatively safely be taken into the body internally or applied to the skin locally, either by inhalation or by way of processed salves. Radon even turned out to be naturally present in the water of thermal springs and was considered responsible for the positive effects of thermal treatment for afflictions like gout and arthritis. Radon – or "radium emanation" as it was then called – became a much sought-after commercial product.

Yet the production of radon did pose a problem. The radium needed could only be created in small amounts. In 1920, the entire global production amounted to no more than 100 grams, and one gram of radium cost 100,000 US dollars. That changed when the uranium from the Shinkolobwe mine in Katanga proved to be exceptionally rich in radium. The Belgian company Union Minière du Haut-Katanga began extracting the radium in 1922, and for that purpose, along with Société Générale Metallurgique de Hoboken, built a radium factory in Olen, in the Kempen region of northern Belgium. The production figures were impressive. From 1923 forward, Olen was already producing 20 grams of radium per year, a figure that in subsequent years was boosted to 50 grams and more. One by one, American manufacturers were displaced, while Belgian radium dominated the global market.

Union Minière involved Belgian universities in its industrial activities. University hospitals were supplied with radium to promote radium therapies. Scientific laboratories were engaged to investigate the radioactive properties of radium further. At Leuven, scientific research concentrated on the analysis of nuclear processes in the creation and interaction of radioisotopes.

That was also the case with Walter Mund, appointed to the professorship for physical chemistry in 1919. Mund was the figurehead for chemistry at Leuven. He had worked with Marie Curie at the *Institut Curie* in Paris. In 1939, he received the Ten-Year State Prize for Chemistry. Ten years later, incidentally, the next State Prize was awarded to his student and assistant Joseph-Charles Jungers – a sign of the lasting relevance of Mund's line of inquiry.

One of his research topics was radon. In 1923, Mund designed a device for producing highly purified radon from a sample of radium. The apparatus made it possible for researchers to work with pure radon, though it was also intended for use in hospitals or sanatoriums that could thus supply themselves with the radon they needed. Union Minière managed the commercialization of the device. How many devices were sold is unknown.

Mund also designed a device for the dissolution of radon gas in water. In this way, thermal springwater could be artificially enriched with radioactive radon, which was considered to have a positive impact on its therapeutic effects. Among other things, Mund's device was used in the thermal waters at the Belgian resort town of Spa, where it was on display for visitors until at least the

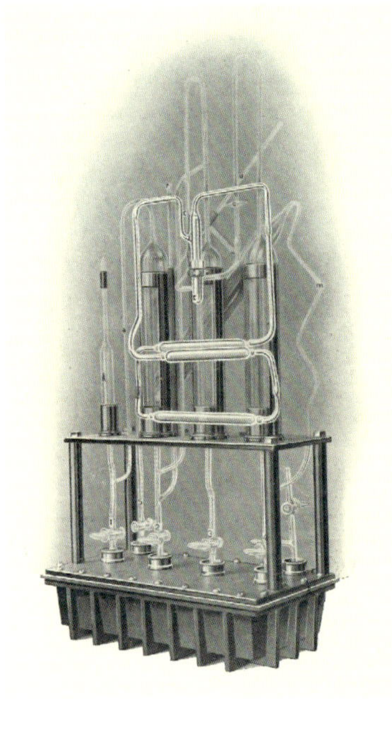

Apparatus for extracting radon, designed by Walter Mund (1925).

Walter Mund (l.) and Georges Lemaître during an international congress in Leuven in 1937.

1950s. By that time, people had already become somewhat more cautious in recommending any radioactive cures.

As a result of the work by Mund and his colleagues, Leuven became a center of expertise in the field of radioisotopes. That knowledge would be useful after World War II, when Belgium reached an agreement with the United States and the United Kingdom on the sale of Belgian uranium. Belgium acquired – after lengthy and difficult negotiations – the means to establish its own research center for investigating peaceful applications for nuclear energy. The scientific leadership of the Centre – today's SCK CEN (Studiecentrum voor de Toepassingen van de Kernenergie, commonly known as the Belgian Nuclear Research Centre) – was entrusted to Professor Marc de Hemptinne at Leuven.

FROM MERCATOR TO LEMAÎTRE: SCIENTISTS IN TOWN

Six hundred years of the sciences have left their traces in the fabric of Leuven. Street names, monuments, memorial plaques, and statues point out the scientists who made the university (and the town) famous. In some cases, they are an explicit homage to these scientists; in others, they are a manifestation of local heritage and tourist interests.

Before the nineteenth century, it was highly unusual for a street to be named after an individual. Only after Belgian independence did the focus shift toward stimulating historical awareness and national pride. The oldest example of a scientist for whom a street was named in Leuven was Andreas Vesalius. In 1838, a street directly connecting the Naamsepoort (Namur Gate) and the train station was planned, though only the first section of it – the Maria-Theresiastraat – was completed. This thoroughfare – called the *rue Vesale* – was indicated on maps by a dotted line. Yet starting in the early 1840s, mentions of addresses on the Vesaliusstraat begin to pop up.

Around the same time, bids were being made for putting statues into the niches in the town hall's façade. Among those images, there were only three scientists: Gerard Mercator; the sixteenth-century mathematician Adrianus Romanus; and his contemporary, the astronomer Cornelius Gemma (son of Gemma Frisius). Among the physicians, we find Henricus Rega, who briefly held the professorship in chemistry and can also be included with the scientists.

The only scientist who was honored with a street name during his lifetime was Jean Servais Stas. Stas was born in Leuven, and studied there at the State University. After a stay in Paris, he was appointed as professor at the Royal Military School. Stas became world-renowned for untangling a dramatic murder case in which the victim had been poisoned.

Replica of the celestial globe constructed by Ferdinand Verbiest for the imperial observatory in Beijing.

Stas managed to localize the residual poison in the corpse and, so doing, point out the guilty party. His lab techniques became part of the basis for modern toxicology.

In 1885, Stas received the Davy Medal from Britain's Royal Society, a very high distinction that only a few years earlier had been awarded, for example, to Dimitri Mendeleev. Leuven's municipal administration took advantage of the occasion not only to grant a medal of honor, but also to name a street after him: the rue du Belle-Vue or Schoon Uitzichtstraat. Incidentally, in the same session on May 17, 1886, the town council also decided to give the widened Lieve Vrouw Broedersstraat (rue des Carmes Chaussés) – which, in part, had already named the Justus Lipsiusstraat – the name of Louis Melsens. Just like Stas, Melsens had been born in Leuven, and had studied chemistry with him at the State University in Leuven, and afterward in Paris. He was primarily famous for a specific type of lightning rod, which protected a building through a network of mutually connected conductors, as in a Faraday cage. Melsens had died just a month before.

Under its predominantly liberal burgomasters, the town of Leuven was not very inclined to honor scientists from the Catholic University. Only in 1894 was a street named after Pierre-Joseph Van Beneden, shortly after his death. By that time, Pierre-Joseph's renown had already paled a little. In his *Geschiedenis van Leuven* (History of Leuven, 1899), an author like J.A. Torfs was of the opinion that the street had been named for Edouard Van Beneden, Pierre-Joseph's son. Edouard was born in Leuven, yet became a professor in Liège. He was an ardent proponent of Darwinism, which many people still contested at the Catholic University. It led to multiple conflicts with his colleagues at Leuven.

At the beginning of the twentieth century, a few scientists were honored with street names. That was the case for Jan Pieter Minckelers and Jean-Baptiste Van Mons. The street names were not thought up arbitrarily. In 1908, the name Minckelersstraat was given to the Koelhem or Koelhemstraat, a name going back to the thirteenth century. Along this street in the nineteenth century, Leuven's first gas factory was located. Minckelers was generally regarded as the inventor of gas lighting. The location of the Van Monsstraat refers to the grounds where Van Mons owned a fruit farm during his professorship at Leuven. In 1833, however, the fruit farm had to make way for Leuven's ... gas factory.

In 1910, a new street connecting the Brabançonnestraat with the Geldenaakse Vest was given the name of Henricus Rega.

University homages remained mostly limited to an academic convocation, to the presentation of a medal of honor or a bust, or to mounting a commemorative plaque.. Now and then, the homage had a more public character. That is how the new medical laboratories in the Minderbroedersstraat came to be named after Rega and Vesalius. Jean-Baptiste Carnoy got a special tribute posthumously. In 1901, Villers College was officially renamed the Carnoy Institute. His name still remains etched in stone on the pediment above the entrance gate.

The most public homages took place on the initiative of the Engineers' Union from Leuven's Special Schools (Unie der Ingenieurs uit de Leuvense Speciale Scholen, or UILv). In 1922, on the Union's fiftieth anniversary, a statue was erected on the Hogeschoolplein in memory of André Dumont, a geology professor and mining expert who had died two years before. In 1877, he first spoke of his suspicion that hard coal deposits would be located in Limburg underground. In 1901, test drilling in the town of As revealed that hard coal was indeed present. The bronze image was executed by the sculptor Paul Van de Kerckhove from Brussels, and the pedestal was designed by Emile Goethals, the professor of architecture at Leuven. At the time of the statue's inauguration,

Inauguration of the statue for André Dumont on the Hogeschoolplein in 1922.

one of seven coal mines in Limburg was already in production. Six others followed in subsequent years.

In 1948, on the occasion of the seventy-fifth anniversary of the UILv, another statue was inaugurated. This time it happened on the Kantineplein in Heverlee, in front of Arenberg Castle, where the new campus was being laid out. The statue was designed by the sculptor Harry Elstrøm, a teacher at the Brussels art institute Sint-Lucas and, beginning in 1952, professor at Leuven's Department of Architecture. The statue presented Jan Pieter Minckelers accompanied by Duke Louis Engelbert of Arenberg. The duke supported Minckelers's experimental research, which led to the discovery of coal gas in 1783. In the same year, a hot-air balloon filled with this gas was launched in the park in front of the castle. In the nineteenth century, Minckelers's gas was used as street lighting on a large scale. During the same ceremony, a commemorative plaque was mounted on the outer wall of the De Valk College in the center of Leuven.

An outlier was the name given to the Ferdinand Verbiestlaan in Heverlee's Ter Elst district. This garden district was laid out in 1955–58, on a parcel next to the philosophical institute of the French-speaking Jesuits. Ferdinand Verbiest was a seventeenth-century Jesuit who, as a missionary in China, managed to climb his way to the position of imperial astronomer. Verbiest studied at the Faculty of Arts at Leuven, though he acquired his knowledge of astronomy primarily as a result of his education within the Jesuit Order. Recognition of Verbiest as an alumnus of the university came about in 1989. At that time, a replica of the Kangxi celestial globe – the one that Verbiest had built for the imperial observatory in 1673 in Beijing – was placed in the courtyard of Arras College (Naamsestraat).

In 1985, on the occasion of the celebrations for 300 years of chemistry at Leuven, the square between Muntstraat and Eikstraat was renamed Jozef Vounckplein. Born in Leuven, Josse Vounck (full name: Judocus Johannes Hubertus Vounck) was professor of chemistry from 1760 to 1772. The name Jozef Vounckplein is unfortunate, though, seeing as his first name

Josse does not come from Josephus but from Judocus. As a result, misunderstanding may arise with his younger brother Henricus Josephus Vounck, who also published on chemistry, though he did not do any original scientific research.

In 2001, a statue of Gerard Mercator, designed by the Leuven artist Raoul Biront, was inaugurated on the Mercatorpad along the Dijle River. This walkway ends up at the Oratoriënhof, approximately where The Castle residential college was located, where Mercator (and Vesalius) studied. Later, Mercator lived in the Schrijnmakersstraat with his wife and children.

In 2008, the esplanade in front of the municipal office building was named for Professor Roger Van Overstraeten. In 1983, Van Overstraeten founded the IMEC, that is, the Interuniversity Micro-Electronics Centre. As , Louis Tobback, Leuven's burgomaster, declared, "He is – as were Jan Pieter Minckelers, André Dumont, and Edouard Remy [politician, industrialist, and philantropist], one of the people who brought Leuven into a new era."[33]

At the College of the Holy Spirit in 2019, a plaque was placed by the European Physical Society to commemorate the origin of Georges Lemaître's Big Bang theory. Lemaître signed his first article about the Big Bang with his personal address at this college, not with his work address at the Premonstratensian College. Two years earlier, a bust of Lemaître by Fred Bellefroid had already been unveiled in the courtyard of that college.

The most recent tribute is the image of Jean Baptiste Van Mons, which was created by Ad Wouters and placed in the Botanical Garden in 2021. Van Mons – internationally renowned as the cultivator of hundreds of new fruit species – already had a commemorative plaque there for some time. Van Mons was of the opinion that 'old' species could be modified by changing their biological growth process. In that respect, he opposed the idea of fixity from Carolus Linnaeus, the Swedish botanist whose image was also created by the same artist and placed in the Botanical Garden.

Finally: in 2001, a street was named in Wilsele for Marguerite Lefèvre, the first female professor at Leuven.

Marguerite Alice Lefèvre, the first female professor at Leuven.

Lefèvre studied geography at Leuven and received a doctorate from Paris's Sorbonne in 1925. Her work found international recognition. The university, however, showed little enthusiasm for including women among its professors. Not until 1960 was Lefèvre named ordinary professor, a milestone (at Leuven) in recognizing female scientists. Four years later she turned seventy and retired as emerita. She died in 1967.

NOTES

1 Letter of Erasmus to Bernardus Bucho van Aytta, Anderlecht, September 24, 1521. *The Correspondence of Erasmus. Vol. 8. Letters 1122 to 1251 (1520 to 1521).* Translated by R.A.B. Mynors, annotated by Peter G. Bietenholz, Toronto: University of Toronto Press, p. 309-10, line 18-19.

2 Letter of Gemma Frisius to Johannes Dantiscus, July 20, 1541. Cited in Steven vanden Broecke, "Gemma Frisius en de Copernicaanse Astronomie," in Roegiers, *Meten is Weten*, p. 33.

3 Gerard Mercator, *Atlas sive cosmographicae meditationes de fabrica mundi et fabricati figura* (Duisburg, 1595), Praefatio in Atlantem.

4 Gerard Mercator, *Atlas sive cosmographicae meditationes de fabrica mundi et fabricati figura* (Duisburg, 1595), Praefatio in Atlantem.

5 Letter of Libertus Fromondus to René Descartes, September 13, 1637. C. Adam en P. Tannery (eds.) *Œuvres de Descartes*, vol. I (1897), p. 406.

6 Report on the compliance of the 'visitation' at Leuven University by Libert De Pape, abbot of Park Abbey, to the governor of the Habsburg Netherlands. Published in E. Reusens, *Documents relatifs à l'histoire de l'université de Louvain (1425-1797)*, vol I (1881), p. 672-673.

7 Arnold Geulincx, *Quaestiones Quodlibeticae* (Antwerp, 1653), pp. 12-13.

8 Letter of Royal Commissioner P.F. de Nény to Duke Charles of Lorraine, March 11, 1755. Cited in Vanpaemel, *Echo's van een wetenschappelijke revolutie*, p. 141.

9 Letter of Joseph Needham to P.F. de Nény, March 7, 1759. Cited in Vanpaemel, *Echo's van een wetenschappelijke revolutie*, p. 146.

10 *Reverendo admodum ac amplissimo viro Joanni Francisco Thysbaert ex Waesmunster [...] carmen* ([Leuven], 1774). Royal Library of Belgium (KBR), Rare Books Dept. CL 5.582 A 4

11 Travel journal of Martinus van Marum, in R.J. Forbes, *Martinus van Marum. Life and Work*. Vol 2 (Haarlem, 1970), p. 20.

12 Cited in A. Felix, "Les débuts et les titulaires de la chaire de chimie," *Revue belge de philologie et d'histoire*, 1986, 64(2), p. 246.

13 Petition of Jan Pieter Minckelers to Holy Roman Emperor Francis II, June 29,1793. Cited in Jaspers, *J.P. Minckelers*, p. 59.

14 Letter from the Faculty of Arts to P.F. de Nény, December 15, 1764. Cited in Vanpaemel, *Echo's van een wetenschappelijke revolutie*, p. 57.

15 Cited on p. 170 in J.D. Schöpflin, "Remarques sur le rétablissement des bonnes études dans les Pays-Bas," *Annuaire de l'Académie royale des sciences et belles-lettres de Bruxelles* 4 (1838), 169-173.

16 Cited on p. 160 in "Rapport du Prince de Kaunitz à Marie-Thérèse, sur l'érection d'une société des sciences et des belles-lettres à Bruxelles," *Annuaire de l'Académie royale des sciences et belles-lettres de Bruxelles* 4 (1838), 151-169.

17 J.F. Dufieu, *Manuel physique ou manière courte et facile d'expliquer les phénomènes de la nature* (Paris, 1758), p. vij.

18 *Jaarboekje der Leuvensche Hoogeschool, voor het jaar 1829* (Brussels, 1829), pp. 81-83.

19 "Sur les Conditions de l'Enseignement Scientifique et la Situation actuelle de la Faculté des Sciences de Louvain. Rapport présenté à Nos Seigneurs les Evêques belges et à Monseigneur le Recteur de l'Université Catholique par la Faculté des Sciences." November 1881. KU Leuven, University Archives. Cited in Vanpaemel, *Wetenschap als roeping*, p. 79.

20 Cited on p. xxii in G. Gilson, "Éloge funèbre de J.B. Carnoy," *La Cellule* 17 (1900), i-xxiv.

21 Cited on p. xix in G. Gilson, "Éloge funèbre de J.B. Carnoy," *La Cellule* 17 (1900), i-xxiv.

22 Cited on p. 741 in P. Martens, "Victor Grégoire, 1870-1938," in *Florilège des Sciences en Belgique* (Brussels, 1968), 727-748.

23 *Gazette de Louvain* (July 5, 1868), p. 2.

24 Cited on p. v. in J.B. Abbeloos, "Oraison funèbre [...] pour le répos de l'âme de M. P.J. Van Beneden," *Annuaire de l'Université catholique de Louvain* 59 (1895), iii-XXVI.

25 Cited on p. 387 in J.B. Martens, "Hoogleeraar Van Beneden," *Het Belfort* 9 (1894), 385-396.

26 Cited on pp. 409-410 in J.S. Stas, "De l'organisation de l'ancienne université de Louvain et de son influence sur le développement intellectuel du pays," *Bulletin de l'Académie royale des sciences, des lettres et des beaux-arts de Belgique* 20 (1853) 3, 401-416.

27 Cited on p. 93 in J. Claerhout, "Driemaandelijks overzicht," *Het Belfort* 3 (1888) 91-97.

28 Cited in L. De Raeymaeker, *Le Cardinal Mercier et L'Institut Supérieur de Philosophie de Louvain* (Leuven, 1952), p. 88.

29 D. Aikman, "Lemaitre Follows Two Paths to Truth. The Famous Physicist, Who is Also a Priest, Tells Why He Finds No Conflict Between Science and Religion," *The New York Times*, February 19, 1933, Section M, p. 3.

30 Lamberts and Roegiers, *De Universiteit te Leuven*, p. 248.

31 Cited in Roegiers, *300 Jaar Chemie te Leuven*, pp. 191-92.

32 Cited in Roegiers, *300 Jaar Chemie te Leuven*, p. 196.

33 "Hand van Prometheus herinnert aan stichter van Imec," *De Standaard* (September 16, 2008).

FURTHER READING

— Brock, M. (2015). *STUK. Een geschiedenis 1977–2015.* Lichtervelde: Uitgeverij Hannibal.
— Coppens, Chr. (1997). *Materiae Promotionis. Natuurwetenschap aan de Oude Universiteit Leuven.* Exhibition catalog, Centrale Bibliotheek [Main Library], KU Leuven.
— Crane, N. (2002). *Mercator: The Man Who Mapped the Planet.* New York: Weidenfeld and Nicolson.
— De Maesschalck, E. (2021). *Leuven en zijn colleges. Trefpunt van intellectueel leven in de Nederlanden (1425–1797).* Gorredijk [NL]:Uitgeverij Sterck & De Vreese.
— De Smedt, J. (1949). "Het Natuurkundig Instituut." *Onze Alma Mater* 3:1,18-20.
— Félix, A. (1986). "Les débuts et les titulaires de la chaire de chimie à la Faculté de Médecine de l'ancienne Université de Louvain." *Revue Belge de Philologie et d'Histoire* 64 (2), 234-255.
— Jaspers, P.A.Th.M. (1983). *J.P. Minckelers 1748–1824.* Maastricht: stichting Historische Reeks Maastricht and Leuven University Press.
— Jeanquart, B. (2007). "Een campus in het groen: de bouwpolitiek van de Katholieke Universiteit van Leuven onder rector Paulin Ladeuze (1909–1940)." Unpublished M.A. thesis, Dept. of History, KU Leuven.
— Lambert, D. (1997). "Monseigneur Georges Lemaître et le débat entre la cosmologie et la foi." *Revue théologique de Louvain* 28, 28-53 and 227-243.
— Lamberts, E., Roegiers, J. (1990). *Leuven university 1425–1985.* Leuven: Leuven University Press.
— Nadler, S. (2017). "The Art of Cartesianism: The Illustrations of Clerselier's Edition of Descartes's *Traité de l'homme* (1664)." In D. Antoine-Mahut, S. Gaugkroger (eds.), *Descartes' Treatise on Man and its Reception.* Cham: Springer International Publishing, 193-223
— Nuytten, D. (2015). "Bouwgeschiedenis en restauratie van het Leuvense jezuïetencollege, later het Veteranencollege." *Monumenten & Landschappen* 34 (6), 30-47.
— Paesmans, G. (1992). "De 18de-eeuwse universitaire colleges te Leuven." *Monumenten en Landschappen* 11 (4), 23-33 .
— Papy, J. (2000). "Humanist Philology as a Scientific Catalyst? The Louvain Collegium Trilingue and its Impact on Sixteenth-and Seventeenth-Century Medicine." In W. Bracke, H. Deumens (eds.), *Medical Latin from the late Middle Ages to the Eighteenth Century.* Brussels: Koninklijke Academie voor Geneeskunde van België, 31-51.
— Roegiers, J. (ed.) (1976). *550 Jaar Universiteit Leuven.* Exhibition catalog, Leuven, Stedelijk Museum.
— Roegiers, J. (ed.) (1985). *300 Jaar chemie te Leuven 1685–1985.* Exhibition catalog, Leuven, University Hall.
— Roegiers, J. (ed.) (2008). *Meten is Weten. Gemma Frisius 1508–2008.* Exhibition catalog, Leuven, Centrale Bibliotheek [Main Library].
— Snaet, J., Verbist, T. (2013). "De grote aula van de Leuvense Universiteit." *Monumenten & Landschappen* 32 (1) 33-63.

In the preceding text, the sections on architectural history have made ample use of the notes found on the webpages of the Flanders inventory of built heritage: Inventaris Onroerend Erfgoed (https://inventaris.onroerenderfgoed.be).

- Staes, J., Vandyck, J. (eds.) (2004). *Hortus Lovaniensis. Vijf eeuwen plantkunde te Leuven*. Leuven: Leuven University Press.
- Tollebeek, J., Nys, L. (2006). *The city on the hill: a history of Leuven University 1968–2005* Leuven: Leuven University Press.
- Van Tiggelen, B. (1995). "La Méthode et 'Les Belgiques': L'Exemple de la nomenclature originale de Karel van Bochaute. In B. Bensaude-Vincent, F. Abbri (eds.), *Lavoisier in European Context. Negotiating a New Language for Chemistry* (Canton, MA: Science History Publications), 43-78.
- Vanhole, J. (2008). "Wederopbouw en expansie. De bouwpolitiek van de Katholieke Universiteit van Leuven tijdens het rectoraat van Van Waeyenbergh (1940–1962)." Unpublished M.A. thesis, Dept. of History, KU Leuven.
- Vanpaemel, G. (1986). *Echo's van een wetenschappelijke revolutie. De mechanistische natuurwetenschap aan de Leuvense Artesfaculteit (1650–1797)*. Verhandelingen van de Koninklijke Academie voor Wetenschappen, Letteren en Schone Kunsten van België. Klasse der Wetenschappen, 48, nr. 173.
- Vanpaemel, G. (2017). *Wetenschap als roeping. Een geschiedenis van de Leuvense faculteit voor wetenschappen*. Leuven: Leuven University Press.
- Vanpaemel, G. (2022). *Towards a Sustainable Future. The Nuclear Research Centre in Mol (1952–2022)*. Leuven: Acco.
- Vanpaemel, G., Padmos, T. (2000). *Wereldwijs. Wetenschappers rond Keizer Karel*. Leuven: Davidsfonds.
- Vanpaemel, G., Smeyers, K., Smets, A., Van der Meijden, D. (eds.) (2012). *Ex Cathedra. Leuvense collegedictaten van de 16de tot de 18de eeuw* (Leuven).
- Waterkeyn, L. (2001). "La vie d'un laboratoire [Institut Carnoy]." In V. Fillieux, F. Hiraux (eds.), *La recherche, passions, pratiques, parcours. La communauté scientifique à l'UCL depuis 1834* (Louvain-la-Neuve), 113-119.

ILLUSTRATION CREDITS

10 Wikimedia Commons
13 Rijksmuseum, RP-P-1940-665, Public Domain
16 Rijksmuseum, RP-P-OB-9419. Public Domain.
21 KU Leuven Libraries, Special Collections, PA04212.

24 Edward Van Even, *Louvain monumental ou Description historique et artistique de tous les édifices civils et religieux de la dite ville*, Leuven, Fonteyn, 1860. KU Leuven Libraries, Special Collections, TA00404.
26 KU Leuven Libraries, Special Collections, ms. 321.
29 KU Leuven Libraries, 2Bergen, PRECA0021.
30 Algemeen Rijksarchief, GR 1078 B
35 Wikimedia Commons.

36 Edward Van Even, *Louvain monumental ou Description historique et artistique de tous les édifices civils et religieux de la dite ville*, Leuven, Fonteyn, 1860. KU Leuven Libraries, Special Collections, TA00404.
39 KU Leuven Art Heritage Collection, Blendeff B271.
40 Museum M, ms. H/16/W, fol. 109v.
45 KU Leuven Art Heritage Collection, Blendeff S268.
46 Edward Van Even, *Louvain monumental ou Description historique et artistique de tous les édifices civils et religieux de la dite ville*, Leuven, Fonteyn, 1860. KU Leuven Libraries, Special Collections, TA00404.

48 KU Leuven Libraries, Special Collections, TA00515.
51 KIK IRPA (CC-NC)
52 KU Leuven Libraries, Special Collections, TA00241.
54 From the photo album Université catholique de Louvain van Edouard Morren (ca. 1900) KU Leuven, University Archives.
59 Wikimedia Commons (Bestor)

62 Edward Van Even, *Louvain monumental ou Description historique et artistique de tous les édifices civils et religieux de la dite ville*, Leuven, Fonteyn, 1860. KU Leuven Libraries, Special Collections, TA00404.
64 From the photo album Université catholique de Louvain van Edouard Morren (ca. 1900). KU Leuven, University Archives.
67 KU Leuven Libraries, Special Collections, PA00170.
71 KU Leuven Art Heritage Collection, Blendeff N00265.

74 Edward Van Even, *Louvain monumental ou Description historique et artistique de tous les édifices civils et religieux de la dite ville*, Leuven, Fonteyn, 1860. KU Leuven Libraries, Special Collections, TA00404.
77 From the photo album Université catholique de Louvain van Edouard Morren (ca. 1900). KU Leuven, University Archives.
81 Private collection.
82 KU Leuven Art Heritage Collection, Blendeff B224.

86 KU Leuven, University Archives.
88 KU Leuven, University Archives, Archive Honoré van Waeyenbergh.
91 KU Leuven, University Archives, Iconography Archive.
96 KU Leuven Libraries, A112979.
97 KU Leuven, University Archives, Archive Mund.

98 Wikimedia Commons.
101 Private collection.
104 From *Florilège des Sciences II* (1968).